A New Playlist

A New Playlist

Hearing Jesus in a Noisy World

A New Playlist
978-1-5018-4347-1
978-1-5018-4348-8 eBook

A New Playlist: Leader Guide
978-1-5018-4349-5
978-1-5018-4350-1 eBook

A New Playlist: DVD
978-1-5018-4351-8

The Connected Life
Small Groups That Create Community

This handy and helpful guide describes how churches can set up, maintain, and nurture small groups to create a congregation that is welcoming and outward-looking. Written by founding pastor Jacob Armstrong with Rachel Armstrong, the guide is based on the pioneering small group ministry of Providence United Methodist Church in Mt. Juliet, Tennessee.

978-1-5018-4345-7
978-1-5018-4346-4 eBook

Also by Jacob Armstrong:
Interruptions
Loving Large
Renovate (The Connected Life Series)
The God Story
Treasure: A Four-Week Study on Faith and Money
Upside Down

With Jorge Acevedo:
Sent: Delivering the Gift of Hope at Christmas

With James W. Moore:
Christmas Gifts That Won't Break: Expanded Edition with Devotions

With Adam Hamilton and Mike Slaughter:
The New Adapters

A NEW PLAYLIST

HEARING JESUS IN A NOISY WORLD

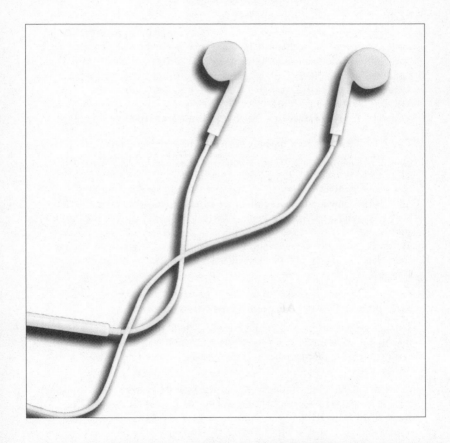

JACOB ARMSTRONG

Abingdon Press
Nashville

Library of Congress Cataloging-in-Publication Data has been requested.
ISBN 978-1-5018-4347-1

18 19 20 21 22 23 24 25 26 27—10 9 8 7 6 5 4 3 2 1

To Lydia—

Thank you for living in such a way that allows me to hear Jesus' voice

CONTENTS

Introduction

INTRODUCTION

When my dad played the Beatles' *White Album* on his old reel-to-reel recorder, the music seemed to go straight inside me. I know now that it entered my ears in waves that were translated into some God-written code in my brain; but that day it seemed that the first guitar riff went into my heart, to a place deep in the recesses of who I am.

It was a summer night in our rural Tennessee home, and my dad had come down from the sweltering attic and laid this mysterious contraption on the kitchen table. It took him awhile to get it set up and connected to the speakers. Having never seen a reel-to-reel recorder before, I remember watching closely as he seemed to be reassembling an ancient machine right before my eyes.

The first song on the *White Album*, "Back in the USSR," is a sort of cold-war parody of a Beach Boys tune. There is nothing particularly special or poignant about the words of this opening track, but it wasn't the lyrics that I remember from that night. It was the sound of John Lennon's six-string Fender bass that thumped my heart into a rhythm I had yet to experience. It was most definitely Paul McCartney's lead guitar that mimicked every Chuck Berry tune ever recorded. It seemed to pump new life into me. The crackling sound of that reel-to-reel tape reverberated off the walls and planted a love of music that has never left me. I can still hear it.

Whatever generation you belong to, you likely have a memory of music moving you and making you experience feelings in a way that was unique and memorable. Whether it's a needle hitting a record or streaming music on your phone, we all know there is power in what we hear.

In many cases, we get to choose what we hear. This is true today more than ever before. Sure, sometimes we are stuck on an elevator during a Muzak version of Barry Manilow (which I realize some people love, and for that I love you), but most of the time, whether in our cars or through our headphones, we get to choose what we listen to.

Recent advances in technology have birthed what is called the playlist. Yes, there have been ways in the past to put together song collections (the mix tape of the 1980s comes to mind), but now, with the playlist, we can choose exactly what to listen to and when to hear it. A playlist can be made for every occasion. We can have a playlist for driving to work, for working out, for relaxing on the back porch. We can have a playlist for the pregame, for the rehearsal dinner, for the campout.

But our playlists include more than music. In any given day, we hear dozens or even hundreds of messages from marketing firms hoping we will buy their products. We hear words at the office that motivate us to work harder or to look for a new job. We hear spoken and unspoken messages from those we love about how well we are doing in our relationships. We hear words from coaches, parents, pastors, and professors. We even hear voices from years before bouncing around in our heads and hearts, telling us about our worth, our abilities, and our dreams.

These words, messages, and voices make up the playlists of our life. They say we have to do certain things and look certain ways. They tell us where to be and when. More than ever before, we are distracted, anxious, and overloaded by the playlists of our culture. They often come in spite of our wishes and without warning.

Some of us are tired of these playlists. Some of us know we can't live up to them anymore. Some of us are looking for a different set of songs to listen to.

This book is about a new playlist. We will consider what it means, in a world with so many different messages, to listen to the song Jesus is singing over us. I mean that literally, not figuratively. Jesus' words are playing over us. They are the most enduring, the most truthful, and the most worthy of attention. What would it mean to create a new playlist that allows us to hear every day what Jesus is saying? It begins with choosing which voices you will listen to. It means opening yourself up to Jesus' words in a new and vulnerable way.

What have you heard about yourself that you just can't shake?

What messages of self-doubt and insecurity have you carried for years?

What would it mean to listen to Jesus, not to the culture?

Jesus has a song for you that goes straight to the heart. It tells you the truth. It's about doing less and being more. He has a new playlist that can't be downloaded on iTunes. You'll find it in an ancient book, in a broken but held-together community called the church, in a Spirit that can speak to you from the deep places of God's heart to the deep places of yours.

Listen up.

1.

Let in the Light

Nov.
7
treats

1.

LET IN THE LIGHT

My mom had me stand on the far side of the kitchen. She stood all the way on the other side of the living room. From twenty feet away she held a page of advertisements from the Sunday newspaper. "What does this say?" Mom asked. "Can you read this?"

I was caught. The jig was up. Mom now knew what I had known for some time. My inability to read aloud a Sears buy-one-get-one-free sale revealed a simple truth that would be a game-changer for third-grade me. I could no longer see clearly. I needed glasses.

In my small hometown, the optometrist's office of Dr. Loyd Baker was in one of the oldest buildings in town. When we arrived, Dr. Baker took me into a little office in the back. With the lights off and illuminated letters on a back wall, he told me I was nearsighted and taught me the meaning of the term. (I know, you're saying, "I thought this book was about what I should hear, not what I can see." Just hang in. I'm getting there.)

After my eye examination, Dr. Baker brought me into his showroom of glasses frames. There were maybe ten to choose from but only two in children's sizes. The first pair, which he called a "Disney Special," had Mickey Mouse ears on the sides. I would risk certain death if I wore those on the Gladeville Elementary School playground. The second and only other pair available was made of a solid plastic that weighed more than most third-graders can lift. They were large. They were brown, the color of mud or something worse. They were ugly. I took a deep breath and pointed at the mud-colored spectacles. "I'll take those."

Two weeks later my glasses came in and I could see! I felt like a new person. That morning I was able to make out the dew on the grass and the clouds floating across the sky. I knew my new look wasn't great, but I was excited and hopeful about the day.

I had been on the school bus five minutes when I heard the first cry of "Four-eyes!" Yep, the name-callers of Bus 129 were no more clever than that—the old "Four-eyes." Still, it stung. I tried to stay strong, but as they came up with even more creative names for me and my new brownish glasses, tears began to form in the corners of my eyes. I'm sure now there were only a few insults, but they bounced around in my mind until they lodged in my heart.

The bus arrived at school, and I rushed to my desk in the front row of Ms. Settler's class. I had been given this special seat because of my inability to read the blackboard. Right before class started, I saw my teacher make her way toward my desk. I dropped my head. I didn't want to talk to anyone, much less my teacher. I wanted the day to be over. I wanted to bury my head in my mom's embrace and tell her about the cruelty of elementary school. I imagined walking into my house and throwing the glasses across the room.

Ms. Settler approached, put her hand on my shoulder, and, in a voice that still echoes inside me, said two words that changed third grade forever.

"Cool glasses."

Cool glasses. That's what my ears heard. That's what my brain decoded. Sure, I was only eight years old, but for some reason . . . I believed those words. I believed Ms. Settler. I believed she was right. I believed she told the truth.

I had to choose that day whom I would listen to, what message I would believe, and how the words would shape the way I was going to live. And third-grade me sided with Ms. Settler. I put aside the put-downs, I let go of the libel, and I let in the promise. I claimed cool. Henceforth, when I heard anything negative about my glasses I had something else to hold on to.

Jesus Sees Your Heart

Jesus said, "The eye is the lamp of the body. If your eyes are healthy, your whole body will be full of light" (Matthew 6:22). There has been much discussion about what Jesus was actually talking about in this verse. He was giving us a metaphor, and, like a lot of metaphors, it can be understood in different ways. I don't think Jesus was talking about just our eyes; he was also talking about our ears and our hearts. He was giving us a warning about what we choose to let in and what we choose to keep out. He was talking about living in a way that we let light in and keep darkness out.

For many of us, thinking about choosing what to take in and what to keep out is more easily said than done. Some of us feel that our lives are headed in so many directions that it would be difficult to slow down enough even to make an assessment, let alone make changes. Think of all the things that come into your brain in a given hour. You might consider your to-do list for the day, the safety of your kids, your retirement savings, the heartbreak of a friend, and what time your favorite TV show is coming on. Think of the feelings that move through your heart. In that same hour you might feel content, tired, excited, frustrated, anxious, thankful, and angry.

In other words, there is a lot going on in your mind and heart—all the messages you're hearing and all the things you feel compelled to do. Assessing and changing those things seems too much to ask. You might think, *If you could just see my heart . . .*

Well, Jesus sees your heart.

Let that sink in.

Jesus sees your heart.

Jesus *knows* your heart. There is no pretending.

And Jesus cares about your heart.

The verse from Matthew 6 about letting in light is found right in the middle of a section of Scripture in which Jesus talks about how much he sees, knows, and cares about our hearts. In Matthew 5–7 we have the longest continuous collection of Jesus' words.

It is traditionally called the Sermon on the Mount, because Jesus said the words while seated on the side of a mountain.

The Sermon on the Mount begins with this description of the setting: "Now when Jesus saw the crowds, he went up on a mountainside and sat down. His disciples came to him, and he began to teach them" (Matthew 5:1-2).

And when Jesus began to teach them on the side of that mountain, it was buckle-your-seatbelt time, because he took the religious understandings of the day—and really the way people looked at their lives—and turned them upside down. It was a breathtaking sermon, if that's what we want to call it, that has stood the test of time for two thousand years. Nobody can touch it.

I think about that as someone who says and writes a lot of words each week. Usually when I go back to a sermon I preached a few months ago, I feel great sympathy for my church. Even in cases where it is a good sermon, it is not a Jesus sermon. Jesus' words become more, deeper, richer every year.

And I am convinced that what we hear from Jesus, in that longest continuous collection of his words, is someone who sees the hearts of busy, distracted people and cares enough to speak into their ears and minds and hearts words that could become a new playlist. Jesus has a new playlist for us that, if we will only listen, can change everything.

Jesus Didn't Keep Walking

If you feel constantly on the move, know this:
Jesus was on the move.

After his baptism around age thirty, Jesus was on the move. He traveled from town to town across the sea and back again, from here to there and from there to here. His days were filled with speaking, teaching, healing, making miracles, and, we would assume, all the normal things that go with daily life. It was during those days that people began following him around— just a small group of friends at first, but then large crowds. At the beginning of Matthew 5, we learn that when Jesus saw the crowds, when he really saw them, he stopped. He went up on the side of a mountain that, before amplification, must have formed a sort of natural amphitheater, and he sat down before the crowds and began to teach. They could hear him. His words entered their ears, passed through their brains, and settled into their hearts.

Jesus was on the move, but when he saw the crowds, he didn't keep walking.

Jesus didn't keep walking.

He stopped. He sat down. And he began to teach.

Now, that may sound strange to us. In our time, most people stand when they teach—behind a podium or perhaps moving around a stage. Often when I speak, I want to get my congregation's attention. I know they are busy. I know their minds and hearts are moving as fast as their lives are. I know they are tempted to look at their phones. So I use every technique I can think of to get their attention. I move from one side of the stage to another. I show a video. I rehearse my sermon until I'm blue in the face.

But Jesus . . .

Jesus sat down to teach. It takes a lot to sit and teach, so we know that the words Jesus spoke carried great authority. But it's not the kind of authority that bosses you around; Jesus cares about your heart. The Sermon on the Mount is all about our hearts.

For centuries, religion had focused on outward expression, on what we do. This, of course, is important. But Jesus was more concerned with the movement of our hearts than the movement of our hands and feet. Jesus taught ideas such as these: "You've heard it said, Don't murder; I say, Don't be angry in your heart. You've heard it said, Don't commit adultery; I say, Be careful what you ponder in your heart."

It was in this context, speaking about our hearts, that Jesus said, "The eye is the lamp of the body. If your eyes are healthy, your whole body will be full of light" (Matthew 6:22). What we open our hearts to can determine whether we live a life filled with light or filled with darkness.

The Last Hours

I have the opportunity to spend time with people during their last hours on earth. It is one of the greatest privileges afforded to a pastor. I stand with family members when we know the end is near. I sit next to bedsides and have conversation, prayer, and tears.

I'll never forget being with John in his last few hours. In particular, I remember the window. It was next to the hospital bed that had been brought into John's bedroom. As he spoke, the afternoon sunlight danced across his face. John had been one of my mentors in the faith. He had a fifty-year head start on me in the ministry, but he treated me as an equal. John was a former marine, a businessman, and a pastor. In my estimation, he had done it all. At the age of eighty, he beat me in a canoe race. He was the one who taught me how to serve Communion. He told me how important it would be to spend time with my kids. I loved John. He was fun, funny, and fiery. And in his last hours, he called me in.

John told me to look out the window. I did. I saw his yard. John said, "Do you see the road?" I didn't but, heck, he was dying, so I said, "I think so, John." He said, "That's the road you came in on." And he began to talk about my journey from where I lived to where he lived. He used my drive to his house as a metaphor for his life. He talked about the movement. He talked about the twists and turns. I don't know if it was the pain medicine, but it was incredible. I looked out the window with him, and I swear I could see his life. With clarity he talked to me about each church he had served, about his time overseas serving our country, but mostly about his family, his friends, and how good God is. He shared some regrets. He shared some mistakes. He shared his heart. John spoke of Jesus as if he just happened to be Jesus' closest friend. We stared out the window and felt the light on our faces.

I preached John's funeral. John told me what to say, and I kept my word. John—who lived an esteemed, distinguished, decorated life, who moved all over the world and had a million experiences—asked me to describe his amazement that Jesus cared about his heart.

I'm going to shoot you straight. I've sat with many, many people before they died, and I can't *ever* recall a time in those last few moments when someone wanted to talk about a beach house, a fancy car, a business venture, or a 401(k). I'm not saying those things aren't important, but in the final moments, what people talk about is the condition of their heart.

They talk about regrets, often about fear, but mostly they talk about their family, their friends, their God, and their heart. Period. Deathbed conversations focus on children who have been taught, nights serving the less fortunate, and relationships that have lasted. People talk about vacations gone awry and moments of great laughter and surprise. They share stories that are amusing and meaningful. They talk about tragedies overcome and healing in the midst of pain. There is less talk about salaries and more about promises—promises shared with God and with people. These are the matters of the heart.

The Difficult Things

Jesus cares about your heart. He wants you to open your heart to his words, to listen to what he has to say about the things that matter most.

Hearing Jesus' words means letting him have access to the difficult things that affect your heart.

In the Sermon on the Mount, Jesus spoke about all the things that no pastor wants to talk about and no congregation wants to hear. Jesus covered it all: worry, anger, lust, where we spend our time, how we spend our money. If you're looking for an easy passage of Scripture to read, stay away from the Sermon on the

Mount. Hearing Jesus' words can be difficult. But Jesus loves us so much that he won't ignore the things that affect our hearts the most. He just loves us too much. Jesus' longest sermon is all about what we let into our hearts.

So, if we want to hear a new playlist, we will first have to come close to Jesus to hear his words. Like the crowds that gathered around him, we will have to sit down and listen to what he is speaking over us. We will also have to be aware of the other playlists that we've allowed into our hearts in our busy, anxious, overscheduled culture. We have to recognize what is playing in our ears when we wake up, when we're at work, and when we go to bed. Some of these messages have become such a part of our lives that we don't even realize we have the headphones on. But we do.

There is a playlist of distraction, schedule overload, and anxiety that is playing loud and clear, and it is crushing your heart. And so I want to introduce you to the new playlist found in Jesus' words. And you can choose to play it. You can put it on repeat and listen to it over and over again.

The playlist of our culture says, "You are supposed to do everything! You are supposed to be all places! You are supposed to say yes to all things! You've got to make everyone happy! You have to run fast, and you have to look good doing it!"

You feel compelled to be at the gym by six, get to the office by seven, work a strong twelve hours, keep the boss happy, get along with your colleagues, hit the grocery store, pick up the kids from ball practice, make dinner for everybody, go to the church meeting afterward, do the laundry, pay your bills online, finish the report, prep for the meeting, watch *American Ninja Warrior* (on DVR, of course), sleep six hours, and then do it all again. And, oh yeah, please make sure to post on Facebook to keep us all updated.

Our hearts tell us this can't be done. Our hearts are right. No wonder our hearts are anxious. Many of us are anxious right now, and it's because our hearts are listening to an unrealistic, ungodly playlist created by a culture that is moving too darn fast.

Simplifying the Complicated

There were people in Jesus' day who were trying to do everything. Their schedules were full, and they were proud of it. They knew there was a lot to do, and they got it done. There were a bunch of rules to follow, and not only did they have these rules all memorized, they bragged about their one-hundred-percent success rate in adhering to them. Annoying, I know. They were the church people.

One of these groups was called the Pharisees. They weren't bad people. On the contrary, their intentions were good. They wanted to do all the things the law said to do. They wanted to be holy. They wanted to be faithful. Somewhere along the way, though, their desire to hear God's words and do what God said ended up leading to a bunch of stuff that had little to do with God. They were just doing. They were just going. At one time the Pharisees had 613 laws that they said had to be followed, 613 rules. Of these, 365 were negative commandments: "Don't do this." Only 248 were positive: "Do this." No one could follow them all.

These days, Pharisees get a lot of bad press because of Jesus' frequently critical words about them. I realize now, though, that I would have been one of them. Maybe you would too—faithful people trying to do all the things we're supposed to do.

One of the things the Pharisees did—I hope I wouldn't have done this—was try to trip Jesus up. They wanted to get him to say and do things that broke the rules. The reason, I think, was that so much of what Jesus said flew in the face of the playlist they'd been listening to.

For instance, there was a rule about not working on the sabbath. They turned that into not doing *anything* on the sabbath. Then they added another dozen rules on top of that. Jesus said if people are hungry on the sabbath, then let them get some grain from the fields. Jesus said if someone is sick on the sabbath, we should help heal them. Jesus said stuff like that, which showed more concern for our hearts than for the rules. The Pharisees hated that talk. They had their headphones on and were listening to a different tune.

One time when they were trying to trip Jesus up, they asked him, "Which is the greatest commandment in the law?" Remember, there were 613 of them. How could anyone pick just one? For a rule lover, it was the king of all trick questions. There was no right answer. What's the greatest commandment? They had him. There was no answer, because their playlist was too complicated.

Jesus took a breath and said, "Love God with all your heart and all your soul and all your mind." Then, without taking a breath, he said, "And love your neighbor." Jesus said that all the laws, all 613 of them, hang on these two.

That's it. Jesus said, You've got 613; I've got two. You've complicated something that is simple. Jesus introduced a new playlist that shook up the religious leaders of his day. It is no less revolutionary today. It rocked the world of the rule-imposing, rule-following Pharisees, and if you take it seriously it will rock yours, too.

A New Playlist: Part 1

So, what would a new playlist look like? To illustrate, let me share a few things that play every day on our old playlist and put them alongside a new playlist.

The old playlist says:

You have to do everything.

You and your kids and for good measure your grandkids are all supposed to do everything. Your kid is supposed to play soccer and softball, be on the drama team, and also be a straight-A student. That's going to involve some extra tutoring. You have to drive them there.

This is an old playlist that says over and over again that you are supposed to do it all. We all feel it.

Here's a new playlist:

You are supposed to do two things: love God and love people.

Of course, you are going to do a bunch more things, but the two guide the many. What if that new playlist began to play in your mind?

I am supposed to do two things. Not everything. Two things. Love God. Love people.

As you get requests, as you get pulled this way and that, you can remember the new playlist and feel the freedom to live into what Jesus said was most important.

Many of us have headphones on that say:

You have to say yes to everything.

If you had attended my church for the last six years, you would have heard six years of stories about softball. During that time, our family had not missed a spring or fall season at the ball park. We spent literally hundreds of nights there, watching and coaching our girls in softball. We loved it. But this year we had one daughter starting kindergarten and another starting middle school. I think I have another daughter, too—it's hard to keep up with. I won't begin to list here the things we are involved in and committed to.

With all that's going on, we decided we would sit out a season of softball. This is sacrilege in our culture, and I'm only kind of joking. It was a tough decision. The league director texted me one last time to ask if I would coach.

"You really aren't coaching this fall?" he texted. I texted the word back and then deleted it. I texted it again. I pressed send.

"No."

As the word went into cyberspace, my daughter's professional softball future went down the tubes. I felt a little sadness. Then a tidal wave of relief. A deep breath filled my lungs. Saying no to that meant I would be saying yes to many things I hold dear. Many things that concern my heart. Many things that for me are about loving God and loving people. So here's a new playlist:

Saying no is often the best yes.

This is a countercultural message, in church as well as elsewhere. You mean, I can say no to my pastor when I'm asked to do the next thing? I can say no to my church about the new request in the bulletin? That's exactly what I mean. If saying no to something in the church frees you to live and breathe, I commend you for saying no (and, yes, your pastor may be mad at me).

Jesus' playlist gives you permission to say no this week, if saying no leads you to say yes to God and yes to loving your neighbor. But some of us would prefer 613 rules, wouldn't we? Jesus teaches us that there can't ever be enough rules for us to know exactly what to do. Life is about love. It's about our hearts being connected to God. It's about loving God and loving our family and loving our neighbors and loving our friends and loving the unlovable, but we can't do these things if we try to it all. So there will be many nos for just a few yeses.

Our world often says:

You have to be all places.

Our schedules are so full. And we feel a pressure to be all places all the time. In our church office recently, our student ministry staff put up a big calendar on the wall—five feet high and three feet wide, with all the student events for the year. I loved the way it enabled us to see everything for months in advance. I said to Allison, one of our staff members who helps me with my schedule, "Can we get one of those big calendars for my schedule?" She said, "You don't want to see it."

We will never truly eliminate our desire to be a lot of places. Some of us like going and doing. But if the playlist you hear right now says, "You are supposed to be all places," here's what a new playlist says:

You can be only one place.

Did you know that? You can be only one place. I don't care how good you are at multi-tasking and compartmentalizing, you can be only one place with your body, and the same thing is true of your mind.

Our church has a number of people who are retired, and they are as busy as the rest of us! We think there will be a day when it all slows down, but it won't unless we begin listening to a new playlist. Activity can be fun and wonderful, but what would it look like to recognize that we can be only one place at a time? And that when we are in that one place, to truly be there.

Jesus had a ton of places he could be and a lot of things to accomplish, but when he saw the crowds, he didn't keep walking. He was there with them. His heart told him that was the one place he was supposed to be.

You're Gone So Much

A few years ago I was traveling somewhere to tell the story of Providence Church. God has done some amazing things at our church, and at that time I was fielding a lot of requests to go places and share the story. It seemed like the right thing to do. It was fun to do it. I felt important in some ways. I'm sure in some ways I liked being noticed.

On one of those occasions, I was rolling my suitcase through our living room, getting ready to go the airport. My daughter Lydia, who was five at the time, came down the steps from her bedroom as I was walking out the door. She had a bag, too. It contained a couple of stuffed animals, a toothbrush, and some pajamas. She grabbed me and said, "Dad, I'm coming with you. You're gone so much."

I thought about all the things I was saying yes to. I thought about how every yes can be a no to more important things. I thought about how I could be only one place. It's true for you, too. I went on the trip that day, but I looked at future requests differently. We all have jobs and obligations. We all have things we need to do.

But what if we started listening to a new playlist? One that says you don't have to do everything. You have to do two things. And those two things guide your decisions.

What if we listened to a playlist that says you don't have to say yes to everything? What if we realized that actually every no is a yes?

What if instead of overloading our schedules to be all places, we fessed up and said, "I am one human who can be only one place." I choose to be home today. I choose right now to be present with my family. I choose right now to go for a walk and be present with God. I choose right now to worship Jesus.

In this day and age it's harder to do these things; I really believe that. I think it was easier in some ways for generations past to be present in one place, to be present before God. But it has always been hard for God's people to resist the temptation of all those rules, because the 613 actually keep us from focusing on the two.

I want to listen to Jesus. I want to let him have my heart. I want to love God. I want to love people. I want to let in the light.

2.

Who Is Your Master?

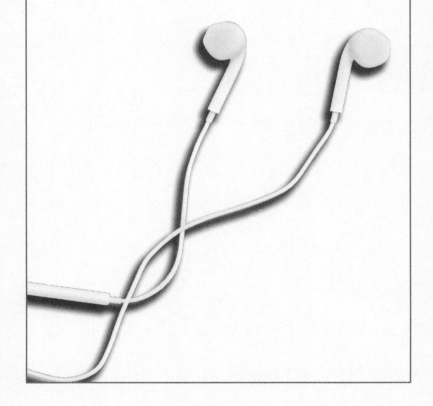

2.

WHO IS YOUR MASTER?

Over the past few years, the churches in our community have sought to stand up and speak out against the evil of racism prevalent in our community and our nation. This has led to conversations, partnerships, and life shared together. One way we do this is by sharing spaces in our buildings.

Our church is mostly white; our neighbor church is predominantly black. Recently a funeral for one of their members was held in our church. He was in his early 40s and left behind his wife and young daughter. He had made a big impact on our community, and the church was filled. The grief in the room was palpable. To be honest, it was audible.

As the family entered our worship center, I noticed their church had a different custom than ours for welcoming the family into the sanctuary. Everyone was asked to stand, and then their pastor stood at the lectern onstage and read Scripture over them. God's word and Jesus' words reverberated through the room and in our hearts. There came a moment when the grief was so heavy that the pastor left his notes, and simply and quietly he began to say this:

"Jesus, Jesus, Jesus, Jesus."

He repeated the name over and over again. The room calmed. Our hearts began to focus.

I was standing in the sound booth at the back of the room, and the repeated name seemed to press me against the back wall. The sound waves seemed to bypass my brain and go straight to my heart. Tears streamed down my face with the simple repeated name that gives us great hope and power.

I wondered, What have I been listening to? What messages and names have I been paying attention to that simply hearing Jesus' name over and over again would almost bring me to my knees?

Then the pastor, knowing that really there were not any more words to say, looked at the family and said, "It's gonna be all right." Again he repeated it. "It's gonna be all right." One by one he looked into each of their eyes and said, "It's gonna be all right. It's gonna be all right. It's gonna be all right." He was not trying to comfort them with a cliché. He was speaking a statement of faith based on the name he had just claimed over them.

I repeated that message to my congregation the next morning in church. We have started saying it to each other in times of need and for no reason at all: "Jesus, Jesus, Jesus, Jesus. It's gonna be all right. It's gonna be all right." It's a different message from the one we hear throughout the week. It's a different message from the lies we often tell ourselves. It's a new playlist. It's truth. But we often miss it because we are so distracted.

A Better Word

Jesus brings us a new promise, a new covenant, a new agreement, and we hear it through the new playlist. The Bible tells me so.

We are told in the Letter to the Hebrews that Jesus is the "mediator of a new covenant" and his blood "speaks a better word than the blood of Abel" (12:24). The blood of Abel represents the old covenant. Cain was the first brother and the first murderer. Cain killed his brother, Abel. Not a good start for our family. Cain wanted what was good for him. Cain was jealous. Cain was focused on himself. Cain shed blood. After Cain, the old covenant required blood to be shed for almost everything. Sacrifices of animals were commonplace and needed for the people of God. There were so many laws, so many messages of what to do that no one could keep up. So, it led to a lot of bloodshed. The people always messed up in following the laws and keeping the messages straight. By the time Jesus had come, the predominant playlist of their religious life had piled law upon law, and no one could live up to it.

Jesus came and spoke a better word. He gave a new playlist. All the laws are summed up in two laws, he said. Love God with everything you've got, and love your neighbor. That's it. Listen to that.

We need a new playlist. Some of us reading this right now know grief in a palpable way. Some of us are depressed right now.

Some of us lost our job months ago and are still struggling to believe that we have value. Some of us are parents who shed tears over our children, tears of fear and anxiety wondering if our family will make it through this season. In the midst of it all, we hear a playlist. I'm not sure who pressed play, but sometimes it's all we can hear.

> *You have to do everything.*
> *You have to say yes to everything.*
> *You have to be all places.*
> *You have to make everybody happy.*
> *You have to look good all the time.*
> *You have to run so fast.*

With these songs on repeat in our headphones, some of us are barely hanging on. We are so distracted by these messages, we miss a simple truth: Jesus is speaking a better word.

Jesus has a different playlist that he wants us to hear. And it's not just a new playlist; it's a good playlist. It is so good, but many of us are too distracted to hear it.

Addicted to Distraction

Recently there has been much written about "distraction addiction." People are actually addicted to being distracted. The most obvious distractions are those of technology.

On the cover of the best-selling book *The Distraction Addiction*, by Alex Soojung-Kim Pang,[1] is an image of a family at the dinner table. Each person at the table, children included, holds an electronic device, and each seems hypnotized by its eerie glow. Even the mom bringing food to the table is looking at her phone as she serves. I laugh, and then it doesn't seem so funny. I see that same eerie glow emanating off the faces of my family. I see how distracted we can be from loving and living, and I know that in my own life I need a different focus.

The need for electronic devices has become deeply ingrained in our culture. Technology is our doorway to information and communication. Papers have been delivered, letters carried, telephones used, encyclopedias purchased. We have always craved information and communication, but now it's at our fingertips whenever we want it. The craving is so deep, we can't shake it off.

We know that phones and tablets aren't bad; they enable us to do some great things, so you won't hear me say to get rid of them. But, once again, Jesus has a better word. He invites me to consider why I should answer e-mail immediately, even after work hours. Why is the buzzing of my phone more important than the person sitting in front of me? Why do I numb myself in front of the TV instead of engaging with another person?

Phones aren't bad, but Jesus invites us to consider: Who is your master?

In Jesus' great sermon, right after he invites us to open our eyes and ears and hearts to let in the light, he says this: "No one can serve two masters. Either you will hate the one and love the other, or you will be devoted to the one and despise the other" (Matthew 6:24).

Jesus tells us about open hearts, and then he warns us about distracted hearts, because distracted hearts can lead to division.

A House Divided

I see division up close every day in my own neighborhood—the type of division where there are two opposite sides with no hope of coming together. Like, it's hard to believe that people could live this close together, could share so many of the same values and history, and yet disagree in such fundamental ways.

I'm talking about a house in our neighborhood that I drive by every day that has two flags flying from the front porch. They are the flags of two very opposite groups. On each side of the porch they have a flag with the beautiful orange of the University of Tennessee, and on the other side a flag with the offensive crimson of the University of Alabama. Living in one house are fans of two warring parties. I once saw a license plate depicting a similar rivalry: at the bottom were the words "a house divided."

That phrase is most commonly attributed to our great president Abraham Lincoln. Lincoln made the phrase famous in an 1858 speech about slavery in America. Lincoln was talking about a nation that would surely fall (he believed) if the division remained. Lincoln began his 1858 speech by saying, "If we could first know where we are, and whither we are tending, we could better judge what to do, and how to do it." And then he said, "A house divided against itself cannot stand."[2]

What most people don't know is that when Lincoln used that phrase, he was quoting Jesus. Jesus said, "Every city or house divided against itself shall not stand" (Matthew 12:25 KJV). Jesus was talking about his heart and our hearts. He knew that a distracted heart becomes divided, and a divided heart cannot stand.

In the Sermon on the Mount, Jesus said the same thing in a different way: "No one can serve two masters" (Matthew 6:24). I can't. You can't. Remember, the Sermon on the Mount is not about politics or money, nor at its core about prayer or following laws or even giving to those in need. It's about our hearts.

I have no problem with Lincoln using Jesus' words to talk about our nation; thank God he did. We might try it now. I have no problem with it on license plates to talk about competing college football teams. But when Jesus talks about a house divided and having only one master, he is talking about my heart and your heart. He is giving us a better word.

Multiple Masters

Our hearts are divided because we are distracted by so many voices. As a pastor, I regularly talk to people about what is going on in their lives. They seek me out and set up an appointment to talk through issues. Most of the time, they don't come to tell me about all the great things that are happening in their lives. Usually they are troubled, stressed, and feeling disconnected. And I have learned that rarely is there just one thing going on; usually they're struggling with multiple masters! We have promised and committed to more masters than can be served—in fact, more than is humanly possible. Multiple masters distract us from our one true master, and competing masters divide our hearts.

We need to get rid of some masters.

The Bible makes a clear delineation between God (big G) and gods (little g). A god is anything we give our hearts to; a god is a master that is not Jesus. The Old Testament and New Testament make it very clear that there is only one God, but there are lots of gods that can distract our hearts. For us to hear from Jesus, we need to get rid of some gods, lose a few masters.

Several years ago I got a new car. It wasn't a brand-new car, but a new one to me and the nicest I'd ever had. When I bought it, it was clean. Like, really clean. At the time, my daughters were eight, six, and two years old. I hadn't seen a clean car in about eight years. I bought new floor mats, and it looked even cleaner. The interior was light gray, and my new floor mats were almost white. I kept it clean, and I let people know how important that was to me. I was the annoying guy who would ask, "Are you bringing that drink in here?"

One beautiful fall day, my family stopped at Sonic to get some drinks for a trip to the park. Life couldn't have been better. These girls are so important to my heart, and we felt the joy of being together. Each girl ordered a grape slushy, the nectar of the gods. At that time, I had made it a year with a spotless interior. (Do you understand the attention and time that required?) It was then that three-year-old Phoebe set her grape slushy in an invisible cup holder that didn't exist and let go. I heard the heart-wrenching sound of Styrofoam splitting on the pristine floor mat. Purple sticky goodness exploded over the back of my car. I was furious. I asked, "Phoebe, why did you do that?" She responded, "I don't know." We were supposed to be headed to the park on a beautiful day, and instead I was in a fast-food parking lot scrubbing and cleaning and muttering. None of my girls said a word, but I could sense what they were all wondering: "When did this car become so dang important?"

The answer? I'll tell you, because it is as clear to me now as it was then. When did this car become so important? When I made it that important.

I have one God. But, I have little gods that I need to get rid of. My guess is you have a few of your own. How do we get rid of them? Say no to multiple masters, and say yes to Jesus. Don't underestimate the power of proclamation: "Jesus, Jesus, Jesus, Jesus." To hear from Jesus, you will have to continually say yes to your one true master.

Who Is Your Master?

One time, Jesus talked about a person from whom an impure spirit had been driven out. Whatever that impure spirit was, the person said no and it was driven out. But then the spirit said, "I will return to the house I left." When the spirit returned, it found the house (the heart) swept clean. So, it invited seven other impure spirits to come and join it for an impure spirit party. The lesson? Saying no is important, but we must then say yes to our one true master. His name is Jesus.

Time and again in the Scriptures, there are moments when people say no to other masters and yes to God. Joshua said,

> *"Throw away the gods your ancestors worshiped*
> *beyond the Euphrates River and in Egypt, and*
> *serve the LORD. But if serving the LORD seems*
> *undesirable to you, then choose for yourselves*
> *this day whom you will serve, whether the gods*
> *your ancestors served beyond the Euphrates, or*

> *the gods of the Amorites, in whose land you are*
> *living. But as for me and my household, we will*
> *serve the* LORD."
>
> *(Joshua 24:14-15)*

Joshua went ahead and claimed it for everybody under his roof. No to gods; yes to God.

Elijah approached the people of God in 1 Kings 18:21 and asked, "How long will you waver between two opinions? If the LORD is God, follow him; but if Baal is God, follow him." The people gave no answer, but for Elijah it was clear. No to gods; yes to God.

Is it bad to keep your car a clean car? No. Is it OK to have a smartphone? Yes. But who is your master? Who is your God? Who owns your heart?

To move from distracted and divided to open and whole, you have to understand your identity, and your identity is found in the one whom you serve. When I changed from wanting a clean car to being the clean car guy, I had a problem because my identity was affected. When you change from being someone who can close big deals to finding your value in the next big deal, beware. When you change from loving a football team to finding your identity in the colors and logo, you are in the danger zone. When you change from being a passionate, committed parent to needing to be the perfect parent who can work, volunteer, clean, and entertain without a hair out of place, be careful. You are inviting a distracted, divided heart to rule over you. And a house divided cannot stand.

If you have such a heart, you will find yourself on a path where one day you will wonder: When did I get so far away from my true master? The answer is when you became so distracted that you listened more to the playlist of our culture than to the better word of Jesus.

A New Playlist:
Part 2

What I'm trying to say is that the main distraction is not our phones, our careers, or our ambition to achieve. The distraction is letting our hearts attend to a playlist that is not the word of God.

We listen to a playlist that says:

You have to make everybody happy.

This leads us to watch for every e-mail even when we should be spending time with loved ones. We have to answer that e-mail because we have to make everybody happy. There is great pressure in our culture to respond, and respond quickly.

Here's a new playlist:

You can't make everybody happy.

Really. You can't. Remember, you can't serve two masters, let alone dozens. Nobody can pull that off, and you won't be the first. I have learned that I can't make everyone happy at church. That's hard for me. I wish that I did; I wish that I could. But most of my decisions make some people happy and some people not so happy. So what do I do? What can you do? Love God and love people. Seek God first, and know that you won't get it right every time, and even when you get it right it won't make everybody happy, because they might have it wrong. We apologize for things where we fall short, but we know we can't make everybody happy.

The playlist says:

You have to look good all the time.

I canceled my gym membership last week. I had been paying for months but not going. When I called to cancel, for some reason they wouldn't let me do it over the phone. I had to stand before a young man at a counter and tell him I was done. I wanted him to think well of me. I wanted to look good. But when you cancel your gym membership, you probably won't look good. If I include the guy who works at the gym as someone I have to look good for, then I have way too many masters.

Here's a new playlist:

You won't look good all the time.

You just won't. Jesus, in his great sermon, said, "Do not worry about your life, what you will eat or drink; or about your body, what you will wear" (Matthew 6:25). If we acknowledge that our identity is in God, then, like the birds and the flowers, we are free not to strive to look good all the time. Our beauty comes from what God has created in us and is doing in us.

The playlist says:

You have to run so fast.

We feel we must move at warp speed, and if we can't keep up, we won't measure up. So we do all we can to keep up the pace, and we are exhausted.

Here's a new playlist:

You weren't made to run that fast.

In Jesus' sermon, he spoke to the hurried, distracted ones. He stopped moving and sat down to try and still the crowd's moving hearts. There are times when I feel that my brain can't slow down. I wake up at three in the morning, and I can't slow things down. I wasn't made to run this fast.

Some might say that our phones are to blame, but I don't think phones are the problem. It's more that we have set expectations based on some playlist we inherited from who-knows-where that is unrealistic and unfaithful.

This week, slow down. This week, be quiet so you can hear. Be still so you can remember who your master is. The master makes all the difference. Our needs and wants find their proper alignment under Christ. You have to know who your master is.

Open Your Heart

Some years back, a little girl was riding in a shopping cart in the grocery store near our house, being pushed by a neighbor who was babysitting her while her parents were out. The little girl saw me walking down the aisle and began to cry out, "Master Jacob! Master Jacob!" She was a bit confused, as she had heard her parents calling me Pastor Jacob. Her neighbor, who recognized me as a local pastor, thought we were a really weird church where kids were taught to call me master! The little girl's parents had to tell her: Jacob is not the master.

Knowing who our master is makes all the difference. Knowing to whom our heart belongs pulls us out of distraction and allows us to hear all manner of beautiful, freeing things God is saying to us. Once we are freed from serving multiple masters, we are able to serve our one true master.

Kevin, a young boy at our church, was baptized recently. Kevin regularly serves as an acolyte. *Acolyte* is an old word that means assistant or follower, and in our church it is what we call the child who lights the candles on the altar table and helps serve Holy Communion. We teach these kids that when they light the candles, it represents bringing Christ's presence into the room. After lighting the candles, they hold bread and juice at the table that signifies Christ offering his life for us, and they watch as Communion is served. Then, at the end, they take the light and carry it out to signify that with open hearts we follow Jesus into the world. Acolytes serve God as an example for all of us.

On the morning of Kevin's baptism, he said no. No to sin. No to other gods. No to living for himself. He said yes to Jesus as Master. Yes to carrying light into dark places. Yes to holding out Jesus to a broken world. Yes to all kinds of wonderful things.

Kevin *loves* being an acolyte. He would do it every week if there weren't other kids who wanted to do it. I asked him why he loves it so much. Without hesitation he said, "Because I get to go to church and do something. I have a purpose."

When searching for your own purpose, keep in mind that it may not be found in going, doing, and impressing. More likely it will be found in slowing, even stopping, and opening your heart, so you can hear the better words that Jesus is speaking to you.

Slow down. Stop. Listen to what Jesus is saying.

3.

Do Not Be Afraid

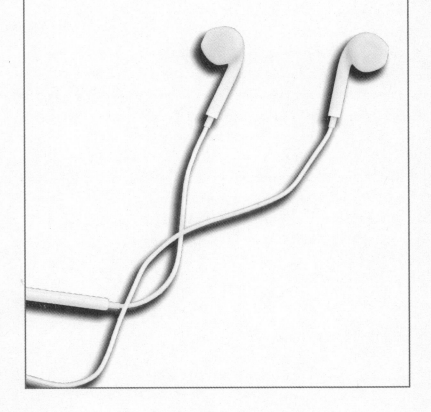

3.

DO NOT BE AFRAID

When I was twenty years old, I thought I had everything going for me. Life couldn't have been better. I had just completed my second year of college. I knew what I was going to do with my life. I had taken a job doing what I loved. I had opened my first bank account. I had rented my first house. And I had bought a ring.

It was hidden away in my sock drawer as I waited for the perfect moment to ask the perfect girl to live the perfect life with me. I even wrote a song for her. I gave it the title, "Let's Live the Life Everybody Dreams About." Romantic, huh?

Even though I was only a few months out of my teenage years, I had already heard the prevailing playlist of our day. You have to do everything. You have to say yes to everything. You have to move so fast. And I was all in. It sounded like exactly the deal I was looking for.

And then suddenly, unexpectedly, out of nowhere it seemed, I became very, very afraid. I'm still surprised, because it came with no warning. I was terrified.

I couldn't sit still. I couldn't think straight. It was as if my whole body was rebelling against my decision to do everything and do it all perfectly. I thought I was embracing adulthood with courage and vigor, but something inside me said, *You can't do this.* And it scared the heck out of me.

One night in college, I awoke in my rented house in a complete panic. My heart was beating out of my chest, and I couldn't catch my breath. I drove myself to the emergency room at one o'clock in the morning. It seemed strange that a twenty-year-old would have a heart attack, but I could think of no other explanation.

I walked into the ER lobby and suddenly felt shame. What was I doing? What was wrong with me? So I left the ER and drove around my college town, all alone, until the sun came up. My whole body was shaking.

The next day I heard for the first time the term "panic attack," as a doctor explained that I was afraid. Not me, I thought. I had everything going for me. I had it all figured out and knew how to execute the plan. But as I began to dig deep into my heart, I knew it was true. I was really, really afraid.

That was some fifteen years ago. I married Rachel, that perfect girl, and now with three beautiful kids and a wonderful ministry, I wish I could tell you that I got over it. I wish this is where I typed:

I don't feel anxiety anymore. .

But I can't tell you that. I can tell you God has worked a miracle around it. As someone who thought I would never be able to stand up in front of people because I was racked with fear, I can report that now I spend my life standing up in front of people and telling them how good God is. But just so you know, I am one of the estimated forty million adults in the United States who admit they struggle with anxiety, which says nothing of the countless millions more who feel some level of stress daily. Anxiety disorders cost the United States more than $42 billion per year, almost one-third of the U.S. mental health bill. Half those costs are associated with the repeated use of health care services by those whose symptoms of anxiety mimic or express themselves in physical symptoms.

You can count me among those who believe in the value of counseling and medication if your doctor thinks these can be helpful for you. But also count me among those who believe in the power of Jesus' words, spoken over you and in you again and again. I know from personal experience that Jesus' words hold great power for the anxious heart.

A New Playlist: Part 3

Over and above all the messages on our culture's playlist, one rings out loud and clear above all the others. It is simple and powerful, and it is on repeat. It sounds like this:

Be afraid.

Be afraid of the stock market; surely it will crash. Be afraid of gas prices; they keep going up. Be afraid of the government; it doesn't have our best interests at heart. Be afraid of a political party—choose one. Be afraid of school; they will test you and test you and test you. Be afraid of the work force; a degree doesn't mean what it used to. Be afraid of retirement; are you sure you have enough saved up? Be afraid of vaccinations, chemicals in your food, toxins in the air. Be afraid of nuclear weapons and global warming. Be afraid of other religions. Be afraid of large public gatherings. Be afraid of serving in the military. Be afraid of going to church. Be afraid.

You might point out that some of these fears are well founded and are based on facts and experience. Or that some are not well founded and are based on fear-mongering in the media. Surely, though, most of us could agree that we hear the message: be afraid. And that, in a nation founded by people of courage, ingenuity, and risk, we are now raising a generation of children who are scared to death.

But . . . people of God, we have a different playlist! A different message rings in the ears of those who love and follow Jesus.

Know what it is?

Want to take a guess?

That's right.

Do Not Be Afraid

Our culture's playlist isn't the only thing on repeat. Some of God's best messages also run on repeat. Such as: God's relentless desire to offer love and reconciliation to those who are far away. Such as: God's continuing call for justice, urging us to speak out for those who can't speak out for themselves. And there are more, a bunch more.

But you would be hard-pressed to find a message from God that is more constant, more repeated, and more emphatically spoken than these four words:

Do not be afraid.

The first time God said it in the Bible was to an old man who thought life had passed him by. The man's name was Abram, which means "exalted father." Abram was approaching triple digits in age and had no kids. His name felt like a joke. But God greeted him one day and said, "Exalted Father, do not be afraid." Then God changed the world through this man.

The next time those four words show up is further along in Abram's story, a few chapters later. Abram had taken God's plan into his own hands and fathered a son, Ishmael, through his wife's servant, a woman named Hagar. Abram's wife Sarai grew jealous, and as a result Abram sent Hagar and Ishmael away to die. Surely Hagar and her son had reason to be afraid. They had been sent into the wilderness to die. They had run out of water. And yet God found them and said, "Do not be afraid; God has heard the boy crying as he lies there" (Genesis 21:17).

God kept saying it throughout the Bible. God said it to Rachel in childbirth. God said it to Joseph's brothers when they feared death during a famine, and to old Jacob their father before he left to join his sons in Egypt. God said it to Moses when he led a bunch of escaped slaves who faced an army on one side and the Red Sea on the other. God said it to those same escaped slaves when they first saw ten rules carved on stone tablets. God said it to Ruth and to her great-grandson David. God said it through David, through Samuel, through Elijah, through Isaiah, through

Jeremiah, through Ezekiel, Joel, and Zephaniah, and—oh, yeah—through Haggai, too.

Do not be afraid is *the* playlist of the Old Testament, and of the New Testament as well.

God said it to Zechariah and Elizabeth, to Mary and Joseph, to the shepherds. God said it to those waiting for Jesus to come into their messed-up, fear-filled world. They were afraid of the government and the economy and all manner of things. God said, Have no fear, for I am sending Jesus to you.

There has always been a playlist that says, *Be afraid*. For that reason God speaks a better word over and over again to the people of God. And Jesus carries on the family tradition of speaking to his beloved and speaking to us: *Do not be afraid*.

What is so important about that phrase?

It changes the way you look at yourself.

Having these words on your playlist is not about just lifting your mood, or changing your attitude, or turning your frown upside down. It's an identity-changer.

Abram, a ninety-nine-year-old man with no kids and a name that was a joke, got renamed Abraham, which means "the father of many nations." God told him, in effect, "Do not be afraid. I am your shield. I am your great reward." He was forever known as Father Abraham, and today the people of three great religions trace their ancestry to him. God changed his identity.

Mary's name meant "bitter." Hebrew moms and dads named their daughters Mary because they were bitter over waiting so long for a savior. Then God's messenger showed up to teenage Mary and said, "Do not be afraid, Mary; you have found favor with God" (Luke 1:30). In response Mary sang, "From now on all generations will call me blessed" (v. 48). I challenge you to find a more revered name in human history than Mary. She was bitter no longer. God changed her identity.

If you open your ears and heart to the phrase *Do not be afraid*, it can change the way you look at and understand who you are. If you hear that phrase today, really hear it, how would it change the way you see yourself?

The phrase changes your identity by changing the way you look at your future. After Abram heard it, after Mary heard it, they looked at their future differently. Because of that, the phrase was also a legacy-changer. People living in fear have one kind of legacy; people living with courage from God have another. God doesn't give us a spirit of fear but of power and love and self-discipline. Understanding these things changes what we leave behind and what we see ahead.

Jesus walked on water to his disciples and said, "Take courage! It is I. Don't be afraid" (Matthew 14:27). When they realized that the one they followed could walk on lakes, their identity changed forever and their legacy would never be the same.

You need to hear it over and over again.

Do not be afraid is not a one-time event. God says it over and over again, because an hour later we will be afraid again. It cuts through all the stuff in our brains and hearts that keep us from being who we were made to be.

My love song for Rachel, "Let's Live the Life Everybody Dreams About," was a little arrogant for sure, but it was written with good intentions. It meant something when I wrote it fifteen years ago. It probably had something to do with achievement and white picket fences—a perfect life with a perfect wife. But in truth, our life together has been something different. It has included tragically losing some people we really love. It has included living with someone who struggles with anxiety. It has included unexpected medical conditions.

Our life, like your life, has been filled with times when we felt fear and times when we wondered where we fit into the story. But thankfully, over and over again, we have heard God say, "Do not be afraid." We have been reminded of our identity and of the One who is our shield and reward. We hope to leave a legacy of love. In our life, we've tried to open our ears and hearts to hear what Jesus is singing over us, to hear a new playlist.

Don't-Worry Songs

It shouldn't be surprising that in the Sermon on the Mount, Jesus' words for the hearts of his people, he talks about worry.

> *"Therefore I tell you, do not worry about your life, what you will eat or drink; or about your body, what you will wear. Is not life more than food, and the body more than clothes? Look at the birds of the air; they do not sow or reap or store away in barns, and yet your heavenly Father feeds them. Are you not much more*

valuable than they? Can any one of you by
worrying add a single hour to your life?"
(Matthew 6:25-27)

I've always thought of this passage as Jesus' don't-worry song. What's a don't-worry song? Oh, they've always been around. Someone takes a few simple, beautiful, truth-filled words and puts them to a tune that we can't get out of our head. There's something about the melody and the simple refrain that walks us out of fear and into a place where we can settle down, breathe deep, and live.

Still not tracking with me? Those of you who remember the 1970s—anybody remember the '70s?—will recall Bob Marley's song "Three Little Birds." You may not recognize the title, but you know the chorus:

> Don't worry about a thing
> 'Cause every little thing gonna be all right

It's a simple song. It talks about seeing three little birds and then tells us over and over again not to worry about a thing. Try listening to it and see if your blood pressure doesn't lower a bit.

Children of the 1980s have only one don't-worry song, "Don't Worry, Be Happy." The lyrics are, pretty much, don't worry, be happy. And if you listen to it, you will feel happy.

The most recent don't-worry song was Pharrell Williams's "Happy." It talks about clapping along if you feel like happiness is the truth. You will find yourself clapping along.

But my favorite don't-worry song goes back a few years before those. It was released in 1964 by the Beach Boys.

Don't worry baby, don't worry baby,
Don't worry baby, everything will turn out alright.

The title—you guessed it—is "Don't Worry Baby." For some reason, when I listen to that song I believe it and I feel better. It's simple, it's straightforward, and it works.

Jesus' don't-worry song in Matthew 6:25-27 is one of the biggest hits on his playlist. There's no evidence for it, but I have to believe that if Jesus had had an acoustic guitar and maybe some dreadlocks, he would have sung this song to the disciples around a campfire. It's the most beautiful don't-worry song that I've ever heard.

At first glance, it seems like some of the don't-worry songs from our own generation—a simple, straightforward message that moves us from worry to a place of peace. But Jesus' song doesn't just make us feel better for a few minutes before going back to the real world. Found in his words are some of the most powerful truths to the most difficult questions that we ask in our busy, conflicted lives.

In the Sermon on the Mount, after Jesus tells us to open up to the light and says we can't live divided lives with two masters—in other words, right in the middle of his words about matters of the heart—he says (or perhaps sings),

Don't worry
Don't worry about your life
Don't worry about what you will eat or drink or wear
You don't have to worry about tomorrow

Jesus covers it all in his don't-worry song.

The Three Great Questions of Worry

As pretty much an expert in worrying, I want to show you the depth of the truth in Jesus' song. I'll do it by giving his answers to what I have called the three great questions of worry.

1. Will I have enough?

Much of our worry and fear stems from our inability to answer this question. In a sense, it's what Adam and Eve were wondering in the garden. It's what Abraham pondered as an old man. It's what the Hebrew people asked during the Exodus: "Moses, will we have enough water, enough food, enough stamina to make it?" It's what most of us wonder on a normal day.

Jesus lists the things we worry about—our lives, our bodies, what we will eat and drink, what we will wear—and then talks about birds.

> *"Look at the birds of the air, they do not sow*
> *or reap or store away in barns, and yet your*
> *heavenly Father feeds them."*
> *(Matthew 6:26)*

Seriously. Jesus answers our number-one worry question by talking about birds. Why?

Jesus gives perspective.

Perspective is one of the most helpful remedies for anxiety. Perspective is an attitude toward something. Perspective is a point-of-view. And often, we can't see a different perspective without someone's help.

When my girls are stressing out over an upcoming test, when tears are flowing at the kitchen table, I try to give them perspective: You've done all you can do. We know you'll try your best. Even if your grade isn't what you're hoping, it'll be fine. We'll keep working. Your future doesn't hinge on this one test. We love you no matter what.

This bird thing may sound simple and trite. It is not. Jesus is pointing out that the birds have all they need, and it's provided by God. And aren't we more valuable than birds? Now, this is not a slight on birds; in fact, just the opposite. Jesus is saying that even the smallest bird in the tallest tree is of great value to God—is taken care of, fed, provided for. And *you* are more valuable. Jesus gives perspective.

2. Will I do enough?

This second question is a doozy for our day. We live in a culture where we are evaluated by what we do. We are given worth by how much we produce. If we really explore some of our worries, we will find this question. Will I do enough? Will I achieve enough? Will I produce enough?

We hear from many people, either implicitly or explicitly, that we aren't doing all we should. Our bosses urge us to work faster. Sometimes our spouses or our parents or our kids make us feel that we never do enough.

Jesus gives assurance.

Assurance is a word we don't use all that much, but it is a good one. A word we do use is *insurance*. Insurance is protection against something that might happen. Insurance is important. Assurance might be even better. Assurance is a positive declaration that gives confidence. You might say it's a promise.

Will I do enough? Rachel and I live out that question, almost frantically at times. Every moment could be filled with helping someone with homework, cleaning something up, getting something fixed, planning for this or that. Will I do enough? It makes us anxious. Jesus gives assurance. How? Look at the flowers.

Jesus sings,

> See how the flowers grow
> They don't do anything
> They do not labor or spin

Now, Jesus is not saying that what we do or how much we do or how hard we work isn't important. He is saying that this core question of our heart—Will I do enough, enough to be worthy, enough to be loved, enough to be at peace?—that question won't be answered based on anything we ourselves can do. It will only be answered through our understanding of what God can do in us.

The flowers that are here today and gone tomorrow—God takes care of them. And God will take care of you. What a promise! Jesus says our heavenly Father knows what we need (Matthew 6:32). Jesus is singing a song over us that is filled with promises that we forget when we try to do everything. In singing it, he is answering the biggest of these three great questions of worry. It's the big question that causes our hearts to tremble. You may not even recognize it at first, but I will explain.

3. Will I be enough?

What we fear most of all is not whether we will have enough or do enough. It is the haunting question of whether we will be enough.

Jesus gives identity.

You may have noticed that I keep coming back to this word, *identity*. It's because the prevailing playlists of our day have led us to believe things about ourselves that aren't true. Much of our worry happens when we begin to seek ourselves in things that are not our true identity.

For some of us, our identity is wrapped up in where we work or what we do or what we've accomplished (or haven't accomplished). For others, our identity is in what has happened to us—a wrong perpetrated against us or a loss we've endured. When our identity is in anything but one thing, we experience anxiety.

Where is our identity? Jesus, Jesus, Jesus, Jesus. In the Sermon on the Mount, Jesus refers to God as Father. For some of us, the image of father is comforting; for others, that image is troublesome. Jesus wants us to see that no matter what our experience of father has been on this earth, we are God's children. And, like a good parent, God knows what we need. God sees our hearts, knows our hearts, cares about our hearts. Our identity is in Christ, so we seek him first, and all the other things are added unto us.

Do You Hear?

On any journey, and especially on the journey with Jesus, we all come to a place where we don't know what to do unless someone helps us, where we are afraid, maybe even paralyzed by fear. You may be there right now. It's at that point when we have to listen for Jesus' song.

Driving home from a family trip to Chattanooga one night, we found ourselves stopped on the interstate. Our daughter Mary, eighteen months old at the time, was in the back seat. She had missed both her naps that day and had not been on her regular routine or diet. As we drove into the sunset, we were praying that she would fall asleep. You may have done this—you don't speak, you don't move, you glance in the rearview mirror until . . . not yet . . . eyes closing . . . she's down. And no sooner had Mary fallen asleep than I had to slam on the brakes as the interstate came to a complete standstill. We sat and sat. It was a hot summer night, and finally I had to roll the windows down and turn the car off. Mary woke up. There was a full-on meltdown—and that was just me! Then Mary started crying, too. Crying and crying. Rachel tried to calm her from the front seat, but to no avail.

Mary was uncomfortable, out of her element, and overtired. She didn't know how to calm down. Rachel reached back, unbuckled Mary, and pulled her into her lap. She then did what only a mom can do. I don't know where they learn it, but up to that point in my life I had never been that up-close-and-personal to see a master at work.

"Shhhhhhhhhh," Rachel said.

And then she said, "Listen, listen."

Mary calmed down.

"Listen, Mary," said Rachel. "Do you hear the bugs?"

I thought, *Do you hear the bugs? This lady is losing it.*

But she knew what she was doing. Once Mary quieted, I could hear the sound of crickets or some kind of bugs in the summer night singing their song.

Rachel said, "Listen, Mary. Do you hear what they're singing?"

By this time, both Mary and I had our eyes wide open and were leaning toward the open windows.

"Do you hear them?" asked Rachel. Then she sang, "It's OK, Mary. It's OK, Mary. It's OK, it's OK, it's OK." We waited in the night.

Sometimes the only thing that helps is a don't-worry song, sung by someone you trust. Jesus is singing one for us.

4.

Rule Followers,
Rule Breakers

4.

RULE FOLLOWERS, RULE BREAKERS

Sociologists say that most people lean toward being either a rule follower or a rule breaker. I'm a rule breaker. My parents were hippies. I question things. I look for other ways. I'm guessing that half of you identify with me and the other half are offended at the idea of not following every rule. Trust me, I understand. I live with a rule follower.

When we were in high school, I had a nickname for Rachel Shepard, my future wife. At the time, I didn't know she was my future wife; I just found her captivating. One of the reasons was her ability to follow every rule and be so good at it. I called her "play-it-by-the-book Shepard." One day I convinced her to skip our study hall lunch period, go down to the lake, and have a picnic with me. I couldn't believe it—Rachel Shepard was going to break a rule! Then, just before we left, Rachel's mom showed up at school and signed her out to go with me during lunch. That was Rachel—she could always use the rules to her advantage. I, on the other hand, wasn't that smart; I just had to break them.

Rule followers, rule breakers. Whichever you are, it's difficult because there are so many rules. Whether you're trying to follow them all or break a few, it's a lot to keep up with. An Internet search will reveal nineteen rules to follow for sure success, thirty-two rules to live a life that feels good every day, and ten important rules for living life to the fullest. There are rules for driving, eating, grammar, and parenting. There are rules for Jenga, *Jeopardy!*, and jacks. Who can keep up? Part of our everyday playlist is a huge collection of rules that are daunting for both rule follower and rule breaker.

In the Sermon on the Mount, Jesus focused on the internal. He pushed past outward actions to arrive at the important part, our hearts. He didn't list a bunch of rules. Finally, though, near the end of his sermon, Jesus did give us one rule. He said it summed up all the other rules about how to act. It's part of his playlist, and it grabs the attention of both groups. Rule followers are drawn to the idea that there could be one great rule; rule breakers are delighted at the thought that one rule would cover them all.

> *"So in everything, do to others what you would*
> *have them to do you, for this sums up the Law*
> *and the Prophets."*
> (*Matthew 7:12*)

Today, we refer to Jesus' great rule as the Golden Rule. It's the highest one, the best one, the one that all others can find their place beneath. It's simple and easy to understand. Treat other people the way you want to be treated.

Three Great Rules

T. B. Larimore, a traveling evangelist born during the mid-nineteenth century in the eastern part of Tennessee, wrote a sermon on the Sermon on the Mount[1] that has stood the test of time. Specifically, it was about the Golden Rule. In it, this gentle country preacher wrote about how this rule is above all the other great rules of human history.

Larimore tells us there have been three great rules in the human playlist since the beginning of time. The first two you most likely won't recognize by title, but you will recognize what they say.

The Iron Rule:

Do what you are big enough to do.

The Iron Rule is about power and might. Might makes right. We can do whatever we're big enough to do.

You know this rule. The person who is biggest and strongest wins. The person with the most muscle, the most power, the most money takes the day. Alexander was called Great, and when he conquered the known world, he didn't do it in diplomatic meetings. Julius Caesar came, saw, and conquered. This rule is old, and it still plays loudly today.

But this rule isn't just for world rulers; it's used in families as well. Cain killed Abel because he was bigger and stronger. Abuse of the weaker by the stronger takes many forms, and we must guard against it in our families.

All of us use this rule from time to time. Maybe it comes out on the interstate when you raise your fist to a car that passes you. Maybe it comes out at the grocery store. I was behind a guy who had twenty-seven items in the fifteen-item express lane. I wanted to smite him. I didn't smite him, but I know the Iron Rule.

Wayne Jackson wrote that "each lock on every door and window throughout the world is testimony to the iron rule. . . . Every corrupt political official who manipulates his [or her] power for personal advantage lives by this system. Bully husbands/fathers who abuse their families are iron-rule devotees."[2]

Many live by the Iron Rule, but it is not the rule that will change the world.

The Silver Rule:
What you do not wish done to you, do not do to others.

The second rule is the Silver Rule. It gets its name in comparison to the Golden Rule. It can be found in Greek philosophy and as far back as 500 BC in Chinese Confucian teaching.

The Silver Rule keeps you from stealing from your neighbor or harming your fellow citizen. It is negative in nature, so it keeps us from action, but it doesn't connect us to anyone or anything. Without this connection, we might sometimes be inclined to say, "It's not my problem," "I'll mind my own business," or even "I'll take care of number one." Nonaction can sometimes be good, but it's not enough.

Silver is good, but it isn't gold. Like the Iron Rule, it's not the rule that will change the world.

The Golden Rule:
Do to others what you would
have them do to you.

Remember what Jesus said when he gave us the Golden Rule? "For this sums up the Law and the Prophets." Which is interesting, because it's the same thing Jesus said when he gave the Great Commandment:

> "'Love the Lord your God with all your heart
> and with all your soul and with all your mind.'
> This is the first and greatest commandment.
> And the second is like it: 'Love your neighbor as
> yourself.' All the Law and the Prophets hang on
> these two commandments."
> *(Matthew 22:37-40)*

So, which is it? Do the Law and the Prophets hinge on loving God and loving neighbor or on the Golden Rule? The answer, of course, is yes. The Golden Rule includes love for God and love for neighbor. Yes. And the Great Commandment includes doing (to God and to others) what you would have them do to you. Yes.

The Golden Rule, like the Great Commandment, is Jesus' rule. And it will change the world.

The Jews and the Samaritans

If this is starting to sound too much like a bunch of religious talk, and you're getting lost in all the rules (even as Jesus was trying to simplify them), then let me tell you a story.

To understand this story, imagine a nation that has two groups of people who are so divided that they despise each other. The two groups worship the same God and have a shared history, but they are not in agreement. They can no longer show kindness, respect, and love to each other. Sound familiar?

It turns out that the two groups were the Jews and the Samaritans. And the story was told by Jesus, who said,

> *"A man was going down from Jerusalem to*
> *Jericho, when he was attacked by robbers. They*
> *stripped him of his clothes, beat him and went*
> *away, leaving him half dead. A priest happened*
> *to be going down the same road, and when he*
> *saw the man, he passed by on the other side.*
> *So too, a Levite, when he came to the place*
> *and saw him, passed by on the other side. But*
> *a Samaritan, as he traveled, came where the*
> *man was; and when he saw him, he took pity on*
> *him. He went to him and bandaged his wounds,*
> *pouring on oil and wine. Then he put the man on*
> *his own donkey, brought him to an inn and took*
> *care of him. The next day he took out two denarii*
> *and gave them to the innkeeper. 'Look after him,'*
> *he said, 'and when I return, I will reimburse you*
> *for any extra expense you may have.'"*
>
> (Luke 10:30-35)

Did you hear the Iron Rule? The robbers were strong, swift, and they took what they could get. They injured, and they gained. The Iron Rule is not enough.

Did you hear the Silver Rule? The religious leaders didn't act. It's not as clear what they did wrong. They didn't kick the man while he was down. They didn't rifle through his pockets. They didn't do anything. The Silver Rule is not enough.

Did you hear the Golden Rule? It occurred when the Samaritan man saw his enemy bleeding in the ditch and didn't keep walking. The Samaritan loved the man. How? By treating the man as he himself would want to be treated.

The Golden Rule is enough. It's the one rule that Jesus gave us. If we put it on our playlist, it can change the world.

Good Gifts

Jesus took the Golden Rule a step further. He told the people,

> *"Who among you will give your children a stone when they ask for bread? Or give them a snake when they ask for fish? If you who are evil know how to give good gifts to your children, how much more will your heavenly Father give good things to those who ask him. Therefore, you should treat people in the same way that you want people to treat you; this is the Law and the Prophets."*
> *(Matthew 7:9-12 CEB)*

Did you catch that? Jesus is saying that we should treat all people the way we would want to be treated not just by others, but by God.

Recently on a trip away from my family, I stumbled upon a gift shop dedicated to all things cats: items for cats, items about cats, items that looked like cats. I went in. I like cats. They had little purses, each one decorated with the face of a cat. The purses had cat ears. They were adorable. I picked out three, one for each of my daughters. They cost $5.95 apiece. Quite a deal—three cat purses for less than twenty bucks. When I got home, I called my girls in and presented each of them with their very own feline handbag. They looooved them. That's an understatement, really. I try not to tell stories where I'm the hero, but in this case, well, you figure it out.

Jesus said that if we earthly parents know how to give good gifts (read: cat purses), how much more does your Father in heaven know how to give good gifts? We think we are so clever and generous. We consider ourselves sacrificial parents. So, if we know how to give good gifts to our kids, what will God give us? We can't even imagine!

It's the Golden Rule, plus. It's on Jesus' playlist. And it's simple—far simpler than the Iron Rule or the Silver Rule, and better.

Living a Different Way

With the Golden Rule, Jesus is saying we can't just enjoy the good songs on his playlist without living a different way. With the Golden Rule, Jesus is calling us to account and telling us what is required. It reminds me of an old tune that would have played in the ears of the Hebrew people when they were in exile. This would have been a part of what Jesus called "the Prophets." The Golden Rule reminds me of Micah.

Micah the prophet asked what God required of him. Micah expected the answer would come from the catalog of things he had been taught were necessary to live for God and be close to God. Micah asked if God wanted burnt offerings or choice sacrifices. In the prophet's words we can hear his exasperation with the mountain of requirements

> *Will the LORD be pleased with thousands of rams,*
> *with ten thousand rivers of olive oil?*
> *Shall I offer my firstborn for my transgression,*
> *the fruit of my body for the sin of my soul?*
> *(Micah 6:7)*

The answer is no. God's requirement: "To act justly and to love mercy and to walk humbly with your God" (v. 8).

Micah learned what Jesus teaches us in the Golden Rule. You can't just enjoy the good religious tunes and not live a different way. Jesus' playlist is about justice, mercy, and humility. It's about treating people in a way that's different from the ingrained rules of our culture.

The Golden Rule begins with God's love.

Before we can be good to others, we must understand God's goodness. You, your family, your coworkers, and our nation will not know how to love others until we know and comprehend that goodness.

This is where an understanding of God's justice is important. This may surprise you, because often when we think about justice we think about punishment. But with Jesus, justice isn't about punishment; it's about rescue. That's what Micah is talking about.

Chapter 6 of Micah is sometimes called "the case against Israel." If you were building a case to wipe out a nation, you would find it in that chapter. Micah lists the reasons why God should be done with the people of God. The rich people are violent, lying is the norm, the poor are taken advantage of. It's why Micah exaggerates what would be needed for them to make things right: even with thousands of rams and rivers of oil, this isn't going to happen. No worship service or big offering is going to get them out of this mess. What will? Doing justice. Treating people right.

Micah is saying that God rescues us even when we don't deserve it and that we should look to make things right with those we have wronged and those who have wronged us.

Several years ago I received e-mails from two church members who had almost the same message. Both had seen a news story on the condition of Native American children in tribal lands. The story said these children were living in Third World conditions. Both e-mails asked, essentially, "What are we going to do about it?"

I didn't know the answer, but we began to talk and pray about it. That first year we sent our Christmas Eve offering to the Clinton Indian Community Center and United Methodist Church in Clinton, Oklahoma. Then a large group of church members traveled to Clinton, formed relationships, and helped build a playground. Then we helped with funding of their after-school program. Then people started going back, some on scheduled mission trips, others taking family trips to check in on our new friends. Then some of those friends visited us and helped us with needs in our community.

As we got to know the people of Clinton, we began to think about the underlying issue. In the early 1800s, the ancestors of our friends were forced out of Tennessee. We learned that initially there were some Methodist people, Jesus followers, who stood alongside native people and said, "No, this is wrong. You can't make them leave." But, then the Methodist pastors of Tennessee called upon their church members to abandon the Native Americans. There were great land gains and financial advantages for the church members if the native people were made to leave. So the Methodists pulled out.

The Trail of Tears runs right through the town where our church is located. In 2014, when our church still met in a middle school gym, tribal leaders and Native American teenagers from Clinton, Oklahoma, stood in Providence United Methodist Church and, as a sign of reconciliation and peace, served us Communion. Something powerful happened that day, and it has led to more justice and even what I would call a few miracles.

The Golden Rule begins with God's love. Once we get Jesus' song on our playlist, we are moved to do good to others. We do justice.

The Golden Rule withholds judgment.

Following the Golden Rule, we extend the same grace God has given us. As Jesus put it, "Don't judge, so that you won't be judged" (Matthew 7:1 CEB). That's pretty clear. The Golden Rule is about justice, but it's also about mercy. It's the same thing that Micah was told: do justice *and* love mercy.

I have a daughter in middle school now. It amazes me that many of the playground games and hallway chants are the same ones I learned twenty-five years ago. Recently my daughter came home and asked if I knew how to play a game called Mercy. It took me a minute, but I remembered. You lock hands with another person, and then you twist and turn their hands, trying to hurt them so they will say "Mercy." If your opponent says it, you win. If you say it, you lose. It's a terribly painful game. You don't lose until you are hurting badly. Not only that, there is something embarrassing about saying "Mercy" in front of your peers. It's a game of physical pain, shame, and regret. Welcome to middle school.

Thinking about it, though, maybe the game isn't so different from how adults act. We grant each other mercy, forgiveness, and relief, but only after we have twisted and turned and ached and then embarrassed ourselves. Mercy, like the playground game of the same name, comes only after a struggle.

Jesus says something a lot different. He doesn't get us in a death grip until we succumb. He comes in a manger. He is born normal, just like us. Jesus walks our streets and experiences our temptations. He knows us. He loves us. He is kind to us. And he speaks rules and shares stories that say he actually loves mercy, gives it freely, and we should love it, too.

Micah speaks to God in a way that shows he expects judgment, and if he has any hope for mercy it is going to be as hard as heck to earn it. God speaks a better word. God speaks to us of mercy through Jesus.

When a woman was brought from a bedroom where she had been committing adultery and was thrown in front of Jesus, everyone knew that she was to be stoned. Those looking on breathed judgment on her.

Jesus, who loved mercy, sang a different song over her. He calmly leaned down to the ground, wrote in the dust with his finger, and then invited anyone who had never sinned against God to stay and throw stones. After everyone walked away, Jesus set the woman free to live a different way. That is mercy.

Jesus' best friend Peter, his closest disciple, was asked by the authorities whether he knew Jesus. With a curse, Peter said he'd never heard of Jesus. Peter had walked with Jesus for three years. He had said he would never leave Jesus, and then, with these words, he did. He just straight up did. When he faced Jesus again, Peter was in a boat on a cold morning as the sun came up. Jesus stood on the beach. Peter knew what he deserved, and yet he jumped into the water and swam to his beloved Savior.

When Peter reached shore, soaking wet and soaking in his shame, he found Jesus cooking fish over a fire. Jesus said, "Come and have breakfast." Then, three times, Jesus asked if Peter loved him, and Peter said yes. Jesus told Peter to treat other people the way Jesus treated him: "Feed my lambs. . . . Take care of my sheep" (John 21:12, 15-16).

That's mercy. That's what Jesus is speaking over you.

The Golden Rule will shock our world. If we begin singing what Jesus is pumping into our ears and hearts, it will get people's attention. It will surprise them with the kindness we ourselves crave. Delivering that message will require great humility, which is the third part of the surprisingly simple requirement God gave to Micah. Do justice, love mercy, and walk humbly with your God.

The Golden Rule requires humbling ourselves.

Getting a new playlist is about humbling ourselves enough to hear Jesus, not those other competing voices. The word *humble* comes from the root *hummus*, a Latin word for the ground or dirt. You can also hear the word *human*. We are mortal—coming from dirt and going back to dirt. Humbling ourselves means keeping things in perspective. Those who passed by the man who was injured by the side of the road were not seeing themselves in the proper perspective. They did not exercise the Golden Rule because they didn't see man as worthy. But humility helps us see everyone the way God sees them.

Where do we learn humility? From Jesus, of course!

Jesus is humble.

Is Jesus mortal? No. But was Jesus human? Yes! There was a song in the early church, maybe the first recorded song in the church's playlist, that is found in Philippians.

> *Christ Jesus:*
>
> > *Who, being in very nature God,*
> > *did not consider equality with God*
> > *something to be used to his own advantage;*
> > *rather, he made himself nothing*
> > *by taking the very nature of a servant,*
> > *being made in human likeness.*
> > *And being found in appearance as a man,*
> > *he humbled himself*
> > *by becoming obedient to death—*
> > *even death on a cross!*
> >
> > *(Philippians 2:5-8)*

Jesus, who had every reason to pass us by, didn't keep walking. He humbled himself for us.

We gain a humble heart by listening to Jesus.

You won't muster up humility. You won't get it in a class or from reading a book. You will get it by opening your heart every day to Jesus' countercultural teaching and letting his words sink deep into your heart. You will get it by doing justice and loving mercy. You will get it by following the Golden Rule.

When we are humble, we live open and connected lives.

When we think too highly of ourselves, when we make our day all about me and pass by others, we close ourselves off. Listening to Jesus keeps us from thinking more highly of ourselves than we ought, and it allows us to be more open and connected with other people.

When we are humble, we can admit mistakes and forgive.

I have trouble admitting mistakes. I think it comes from living in a land where the Iron Rule and the Silver Rule are often lifted higher than the Golden Rule. I will be three minutes into a conversation bordering on a disagreement, and I'll realize that if I would just humble myself and admit my own wrong, we could make a lot of progress. If I would just say that I spoke out of turn or that my words led to a problem in the first place, everything would go better.

But for some reason I can't do that. I keep being defensive. I keep seeking the upper hand. I keep trying to be stronger, or I respond with inaction. The reason I do it is because humility is not deep in my heart. I haven't been listening to Jesus nearly enough. If you are finding it difficult to forgive or admit a mistake, it may have less to do with the other person and more do to what your heart is listening to.

When we are humble, we can reflect and celebrate.

With the world's playlist, it's hard to slow down. You have to get up super early and hit the ground running. You have to fall asleep with all the stuff still swirling in your head. Listening to Jesus means allowing the pace to be slowed down. To pray, to think about God, involves stopping when others keep walking.

In moments when I would usually be moving fast, I'm trying to stop and listen. The faster I move, the more I think the world is resting on my shoulders. When Micah asked what was required, God didn't say to do justice, love mercy, and run the fifty-yard dash with your God. Nope, walk humbly.

My middle daughter, Lydia, is a sprinter. She has run in an annual countywide track competition, and her best event is the hundred-yard dash. Last year, she did well and set a goal to do better this year. We began to work on sprints together in front of our house. I told her, "You've got to put it all out there. You should feel like throwing up after crossing the finish line."

Well, that advice may work for the hundred-yard dash, but I hope to teach her a different pace for her life. A pace that comes from the rhythm of Jesus' words. A pace that allows her to reflect, to celebrate the things God has done and celebrate other people.

Do you ever find it difficult to celebrate what others have done? You hear of something great that a friend or colleague has done, and somehow it bothers you? That's not an achievement problem; it's a heart problem.

When we are humble, we can release control and be lifted up.

Some of us are holding on so tight. Pay attention to your hands right now. Are you gripping tightly, either physically or emotionally? Open your hands. Release control. It comes with being humble. It comes by letting Jesus' voice be louder than yours.

And then, guess what? If you lower yourself, Jesus doesn't leave you on the ground. He will lift you up. In that church song in Philippians 2, Jesus humbles himself to the point of death, but God exalts him to the highest place. That same thing can happen to us. The Golden Rule is about lowering ourselves, and when we do, God lifts us up. It's about justice. It's about mercy. It's about humility. It's about life.

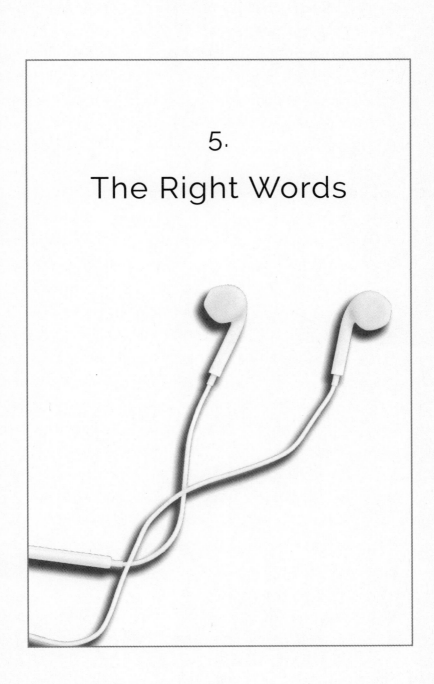

5.

The Right Words

5.

THE RIGHT WORDS

So many words.

We hear thousands and thousands of words every day. So many that won't amount to anything. So many that will never be remembered. We hear the words. They go in one ear and out the other.

We also say thousands of words. Some of them we craft and rehearse in our minds a hundred times before saying them. Some of them we speak with seemingly no thought at all. Some of them we wish we could take back. Some of them make us wonder where they came from.

Sometimes the words we say don't seem to mean anything. But other times, the words we say seem to mean everything.

Some words matter. Some words, spoken by the right person at the right time in the right place, can change everything.

You don't believe me?

Last Saturday night I stood in front of a man and woman and said to the people gathered there, "I announce to you that they are husband and wife." That's it. I do it all the time. Imagine that—if I string together the right words at the right time and place, the people walk away from me thinking they are married! And what's crazier than that, they are!

Recently, my friends Chris and Erica stood before a judge. They held a little boy that they picked up in a hospital in Florida. The judge said some words, and that little boy, David, became their son. I was with them after that day. Little David was in the carrier, little David cried, little David was rocked to sleep. Whatever that judge said, it worked. I can testify that little David is their son.

It Happens in the Heart

It's not the words of a pastor that make a marriage. It's not a judge's proclamation that makes a boy become a treasured son in a family. These are things that happen in the heart. The words, the confession, and the testimony do something to seal the promise in our hearts. They make public a mystery that no words could ever capture. But we need the words.

The right words hold great power.

I returned recently to the place where Rachel and I were married, First United Methodist Church in Murfreesboro, Tennessee. It had been about fifteen years since we said words to seal our promise. The building, though, is no longer First United Methodist Church. It's a bank. In fact, the bank only uses the parts of the old church building that used to be classrooms and a gym. The sanctuary where Rachel and I were married has been untouched now for over ten years.

I sneaked back in. The pews had been pulled out. The carpet was tattered, and the paint was peeling off the walls. But I felt it. I felt the power of two hundred years of prayer. I could almost hear the hymns echoing off the back wall. I remembered my first sermon as a United Methodist pastor, in that very room— how nervous I was, how bad it was, how the people urged me on with smiles and nods. I remembered my wedding day. My beautiful bride walking down an aisle. My stammering words. We made a promise in that room with simple words, and our pastor announced that we were husband and wife, in the name of the Father and of the Son and of the Holy Spirit. Those whom God has joined together let no one separate.

Old words in old places can still hold great power for today.

In this book, we've been trying to listen to some old words that were spoken from the side of a hill in a land far, far away. Sometimes we have to strain our ears just to make out the ancient words in our noisy world. But Jesus' words are worth listening to, paying attention to, and sealing into our hearts. So we keep listening, and we keep speaking in response.

Jesus followers have been listening and speaking for a long time now. There are some things that we think are essential to hear and say. After Jesus ascended to heaven, the church was formed by the power of the Holy Spirit, and the people who became known as Christians started to string together phrases to hold the promises of their new faith. They spent years agreeing upon and fighting over statements they called *confessions* or *creeds* that they would repeat over and over again. Some of these phrases are still repeated today. We could say, "Old words, who cares?" But there is something in us that pays attention to words that were repeated in homes and hidden on scrolls, words that people gave their lives to get to us.

One of the simplest and most repeated confessions of the early followers of Christ was "Jesus is Lord." That little phrase was really the first statement of belief for the church. Christians were even known to use the phrase as a greeting. Paul wrote in his letter to the Romans, "If you declare with your mouth, 'Jesus is Lord,' and believe in your heart that God raised him from the dead, you will be saved" (Romans 10:9). The next verse spins it around a bit: "For it is with your heart that you believe and are justified, and it is with your mouth that you profess your faith and are saved" (v. 10).

Put together, these two verses lead us to understand a rhythm of what we hear, believe, and say. Belief and confession. Confession and belief. Not one or the other, but both. Just listening and believing is not enough. Just speaking without believing is not enough. And in either case, it's not enough just to do it once. For me, this is where Jesus' playlist comes in.

Imagine if all we needed was to hear from Jesus one time, to believe what he said one time, and to make our confession one time. Then we could move on with our life. We wouldn't have to listen to Jesus' words every day. Romans 10:9 is often used to help people mark their salvation moment, and rightly so. Do you want to be saved? Do you believe in Jesus? Do you confess him as Lord? Yes? Then, you are saved!

But the early Christians said "Jesus is Lord" every time they saw each other. They established creeds and patterns for proclaiming, and they said these over and over again.

That's why I would adjust my statement about the power of words spoken to say this:

The right words with the same people
in the same place over and over again
hold great power.

It's longer, but I like it better. We listen to Jesus over and over again, like we do music on a playlist. His songs become the songs we sing. And the first song, one of belief, is a confession of Jesus as Lord. Our Lord. My Lord. Master, Savior, Lord.

The creeds, whether short or long, are packed with meaning. After all, confessing Jesus as Lord is a lot to believe. In the Apostles' Creed, the confession of Jesus as Lord includes belief in virgin birth, ascension to heaven, and plenty more in between! A student asked one of my seminary professors, "What if I'm having a day or season when I just don't believe part of our creeds?" He answered, "That's all right. We'll believe it for you." If you struggle with some part of what Christians believe, if you can't say it all every day, welcome to the club. We say what we believe over and over again, and there may be some days we are saying it for you. There will be days when we need you to say it for us. So the new playlist is not just about hearing Jesus' song in your heart; it's about saying it. We believe it and we say it. We say it and we believe it.

My daughter Phoebe and I have a ritual for school drop. When we hit the backed-up line of cars coming out of the school driveway, we turn off the radio. We sit quiet for a moment, and then I put my hand in the back seat. She grabs it. We say a prayer. It's a prayer her mom and I wrote when we were first married. I had begun studies at an Episcopal seminary where liturgy and ritual where emphasized, and our hearts had connected with the repetition of confessional words spoken at the same time and place by the same people over and over again. We wrote a simple morning prayer that we said together before we left for work and school, and that's the prayer Phoebe and I say:

> O God, this day we praise you for our life and we commit our lives to you. We thank you for our Lord Jesus who gives us passion and purpose. Lead us this day by your Holy Spirit to be faithful to you and faithful to each other. Forgive us of our sins and renew us to new life in you. We believe by faith that you alone will sustain us today. Hold us safe until we are together again. Amen.

When we say amen, Phoebe lets go of my hand, but I hold on to hers. We play a little game where she tries to wriggle her hand out of mine, and she is always successful. As we round the corner and see the school drop-off, Phoebe then, every morning, says, "Welcome to the torture chamber." You just have to know Phoebe, I guess. Then, right before she gets out, she says, "I love you." And I say, "I love you, too." And then she says, "Don't forget to wave," and I say, "I never forget to wave." Then she gets out and, with the solemn look of someone going into battle, she turns with no smile and waves. Every morning, every day. Every morning, every day.

Confession and belief. Belief and confession. There is power in saying the same things with the same people in the same place over and over again.

Name-Droppers

In hearing and speaking Jesus' song over and over again, we become name-droppers of the most powerful name.

If you aren't familiar with the term, *name-dropping* is casually mentioning a famous or cool or notable person so as to appear vicariously famous or cool or notable yourself. It happens on the red carpet, in middle school, on social media. American essayist Joseph Epstein defines name-dropping as "using the magic that adheres to the names of celebrated people to establish one's superiority while at the same time making the next person feel the drabness of his or her own life."[1]

It's funny how someone's name, dropped at the right time in the right way, can hold power in a conversation. In a sense, we've been talking about dropping Jesus' name as we confess him as Lord. But this kind of name-dropping can be misused.

In the Sermon on the Mount, Jesus said, "Not everyone who says to me, 'Lord, Lord,' will enter the kingdom of heaven, but only the one who does the will of my Father who is in heaven" (Matthew 7:21). This doesn't lessen the importance of confession, but it does increase the importance of listening to Jesus. It's not enough to be a Jesus name-dropper; we must listen to his words and live in accordance with what he says. This Scripture is a warning to those of us who, marching to the tune of a different playlist, say Jesus' name without a connection to our hearts.

I'm curious, then, how we can drop Jesus' name in a way that's not empty and contrived, but that leads more people to hear his voice. Isaiah has something to say about this. Yeah, Isaiah, who lived eight centuries before Jesus. Isaiah describes a day that's coming when the people of God will get their feet on solid ground, vanquish their enemies, and make things right with God. Isaiah talks about what the people will sing in light of what God is singing over them.

> *In that day this song will be sung in the land of*
> *Judah. . . .*
>
> *Yes, LORD, walking in the way of your laws,*
> *   we wait for you;*
> *your name and renown*
> *   are the desire of our hearts.*
> (Isaiah 26:1a, 8)

Did you hear it at the end of the song? God's name and renown are the desire of our hearts. God's name and renown are the desire of our hearts. (Say that again!) God's name and renown are the desire of our hearts.

The playlist of our culture is about making our name famous. But God's people sing a song that make God's name famous.

The Name and Fame of God

At one of the first gatherings when we began to dream about what would become Providence Church, we had a simple exercise in which we spoke our hopes for what would happen with the new church in ten years. The church was just forming, but we asked folks to dream about what they hoped people might say after we had been around a decade or so.

Someone said, "My hope is that in ten years, something so amazing has happened that we would have to say, 'God did it.'"

As we approach our tenth year, we have uttered that phrase countless times to give thanks, credit, and praise to God. When we would have been tempted to stick out our chests and take all the credit, we have sought to drop God's name. If we had been listening to a different playlist, we certainly would have said it was all about us.

The name I'm best at dropping, of course, is mine. When I've done something, I want people to know. I can try to be subtle, I can put on false modesty, but the desire is the same. I want people to know I did something. I want to be noticed. I wonder how Alexander got the name Alexander the Great. I just wonder if he had something to do with it. "Um, guys, I'm changing my last name. Yeah, changing it to the Great." I wonder if Alexander came up with that.

When we listen to Jesus' playlist in the Sermon on the Mount, we realize that one reason we exist is to point others to God. Like the people of God in Isaiah's day, we find that the desire of our hearts is the name and fame of God. The culture's playlist tells us the exact opposite, but we know there is joy in doing what our hearts were made to do. As we take the attention off who we are and instead point people to God, we experience a contentment that is not found in the pursuit of personal fame.

The new playlist—listening to God's word over the din of the world's noise—leads us to a new place of trust. It's a place where we can let go of our incessant desire to make people notice us and speak our names. It's a place where we don't have to follow every whim that's blown our way by the winds of culture. It means letting God's word seep into a deep place in our hearts, where we can hear what Jesus is saying even when those winds become a storm.

Memory Verses

I memorized a couple of verses when I was in college and struggling with anxiety. It was the first time in my life that I couldn't sleep at night. I was so anxious that when I tried to rest, the noise in my brain and heart got louder. I would speak these verses in my bedroom at night, giving voice to promises I had yet to experience. One of the verses was from Philippians, where Paul says,

> *Do not be anxious about anything, but in*
> *every situation, by prayer and petition, with*
> *thanksgiving, present your requests to God.*
> *And the peace of God, which transcends all*
> *understanding, will guard your hearts and your*
> *minds in Christ Jesus.*
>
> *(Philippians 4:6-7)*

I've said that verse a thousand times in my heart and out loud in the dark. It became my theme song for that time in my life. Even today, when I get still, it bubbles up in my heart.

The other verse that I claimed in those days was from Proverbs. Eugene Peterson notes that as you read Proverbs you can get easily get overwhelmed with detail. He notes that Proverbs is "a collection of more than five hundred separate aphorisms polished into pungent sentences." Peterson asks, "Can you imagine what it is like to have five hundred proverbs dumped on you?"[2]

I think we feel that way sometimes even with Jesus' playlist. The Bible is so big, and sometimes it's overwhelming in an overwhelming life to figure out what the collection of sayings, history, and wisdom is saying to us. But I encourage you not to give up, to keep listening and reading, because often one sentence rises out of it to become *the* song you need to sing. That's what happened to me with Proverbs 3:5-6. In the middle of the night, this four-part proverb pulled me out of the darkness. It was a way for me to drop a bigger name into the struggle, and the name of the Lord held more power than I ever imagined.

As a twenty-year-old, I would lie on my back and say to the ceiling,

> *Trust in the* LORD *with all your heart*
>   *and lean not on your own understanding;*
> *in all your ways submit to him,*
>   *and he will make your paths straight.*

And here's a little secret. I still say those verses at night. Regularly. The other night, I was lying there in the dark saying it. Barely audible, so as not to wake my bride with my recitation of Scripture. That's how preachers roll. "What was that, honey?" "Oh, just speaking God's word into the night. Go back to your slumber." Seriously, I was so anxious that I couldn't sleep. My mind raced with today's regrets and tomorrow's deadlines, and I spoke the Scriptures that have become like old friends.

"Trust in the LORD. . . ." As I recited that Scripture in the dark, it hit me. I was name-dropping. I was bringing God's name into the room, and it was the desire of my heart. I was no different than those to whom Isaiah was talking. I needed my feet on solid ground, my enemies vanquished, and things to be right with God. And so, rightly, I called upon the Lord. The word *LORD* in that Scripture is actually *Yahweh*, the very name of God. Don't underestimate what happens when you make the Lord not just the playlist in your heart, but the confession of your mouth. God wants to win our hearts, and one indicator is what comes out of our mouths.

"Trust in the LORD with all your heart," I said. But how much did I really trust God? How much do you really trust God? Trust isn't about a feeling, so even when I'm feeling anxious, my heart continues to trust. Trust won't come naturally, so I don't have to feel shame because I'm on the tightrope of worry.

Trusting God

Remember, Jesus says the playlist of our life is to love God and love neighbor. When Jesus tells us to love God, he is quoting a verse from Deuteronomy that says, "Love the LORD your God with all your heart and with all your soul and with all your strength" (6:5). Again, the word *LORD* here is *Yahweh*, the name of God. There are many kinds of gods, so this verse specifically names Yahweh.

But God's name is not the only thing revealed by this Scripture's terminology. The Hebrew word for *love* in this verse means "to be loyal to." When Jesus tells us that the most important thing we can do is love God, he's not talking about a feeling. It's about loyalty. It's about trust. Jesus is referring to the choices we make every day, every hour, every minute.

I talk to people all the time in some kind of relationship, often marriage, who are struggling. They tell me, "I just don't feel it anymore" or "I'm not in love anymore." I get it. Life can end up a lot different than it was when you first experienced the feelings. But relationships are about much more than feelings, including your relationship with God. Dropping God's name into a situation, even when you don't feel God's presence, is completely appropriate and acceptable and needed! It is an action of trust! It is a choice that honors the relationship.

And when we trust God, we find God to be trustworthy.

When we listen to the culture's playlist to do it all, be everywhere, and please everyone, we are leaning on our own understanding. We are leaning on what we can see and make sense of. That's what comes naturally. But achieving a deeper trust requires a hard lean onto God.

I hope someday you'll be able to meet Zeke. He is our 110-pound golden retriever. (So, he has a bit of a weight problem. Don't bring it up. He's sensitive about it.) When I was a kid, I had a golden retriever named Zeke, and so when our girls were old enough, we got them a golden retriever named Zeke.

Zeke is a hard leaner. If you come to our house (and consider this an invitation, but not all at once and not unannounced), you will not have to earn Zeke's trust. He is not a guard dog. When you pull up, you are a part of the family. He will lean on you. As you try to exit your car, he will lean onto your leg. As you try to stand, he is likely to make you lose your balance. I love that about Zeke. He leans hard.

God is looking for you to lean like Zeke. God wants you to take some pressure off your own understanding (because you can't understand everything) and lean. Press in. Lean hard. God will not be shaken.

There's an old church song that was on the playlist of the twentieth-century church, especially in rural areas. It is called "Leaning on the Everlasting Arms" and was written in 1887 by Anthony J. Showalter and Elisha A. Hoffman. Showalter was a music teacher in Dalton, Georgia. One day he received a letter from one of his former students. The student's wife had died, and the student was of course distraught. Showalter, too, was distraught for his beloved student. He wrote back to the student and quoted an obscure verse from Deuteronomy: "The eternal God is *thy* refuge, and underneath *are* the everlasting arms" (Deuteronomy 33:27 KJV). Based on that verse, Showalter wrote the refrain and asked Hoffman to write the stanzas.

> What a fellowship, what a joy divine,
> leaning on the everlasting arms;
> what a blessedness, what a peace is mine,
> leaning on the everlasting arms.
> Leaning, leaning,
> safe and secure from all alarms;
> leaning, leaning,
> leaning on the everlasting arms.

Maybe you aren't ready to trust with all your heart. I get that. Some of us have been burned big-time by trusting others. You might even feel that way about God. But would you start to lean? Lean away from your own understanding and lean toward God. As you lean, you will be able to hear a different playlist. It is a better one.

You know what that means. Speak his name. Use his name at work, in your home, in your church. Talk about it in the car _____ marriage. Teach it to your kids or

_____ that God will make your _____ the most famous Proverb, _____ aighter. And while that part _____ of the verse. The best part _____ od's will allows us to make _____ e it not be an empty song. _____ ic day when our paths are _____ atically, so that God's being _____ r being famous. It happens _____ g, when we speak the most powerful name _____ hts.

So, give it a try. Drop his name and see what happens. Jesus, Jesus, Jesus, Jesus.

6.

The Power
of Connection

6.

THE POWER
OF CONNECTION

The Sermon on the Mount ends with these words from Jesus:

*"Therefore everyone who hears these words
of mine and puts them into practice is like a
wise man who built his house on the rock. The
rain came down, the streams rose, and the
winds blew and beat against that house; yet it
did not fall, because it had its foundation on
the rock. But everyone who hears these words
of mine and does not put them into practice is
like a foolish man who built his house on sand.
The rain came down, the streams rose, and the
winds blew and beat against that house, and it
fell with a great crash."*

(Matthew 7:24-27)

We have imagined what it would be like to hear Jesus' song on a new playlist and let it sink deep into our hearts. As Jesus closed his great sermon, he gave us a pretty clear image of what it will look like if we do this, and what it will look like if we don't.

I grew up in a small town outside Nashville, Tennessee, before Nashville became a fast-growing metropolis and worldwide tourist destination. Even back then it was known as the country music capital, and just outside of Nashville was, well, the country. So, full disclosure, I was a member of 4-H and at one time was the president of our high school's chapter of the Future Farmers of America. Those organizations taught me a lot about leadership, public speaking, and soil. For years I was taught about soil and even judged soil. I was a teenage expert on dirt.

You may not think much about dirt, but it has a lot to do with agriculture and also with water conservation, public health, and building. In fact, Jesus ended his great sermon with a soil metaphor, using an image that his hearers would understand about the type of ground that you build on. He said, basically, if you hear my words and put them into practice, it's like building your life on solid ground. If you hear my words and choose to follow a different playlist, it's like building your life on sand. Well, take it from a former FFA soil judger, building on sand is not a good idea.

In using that image, Jesus was not giving construction advice as much as he was talking about connection. He was reminding us that nothing is more important than what our lives are built on and connected to. And the way we assure ourselves of firm foundations and healthy connections is by hearing his words and putting them into practice.

What does it mean to build your life on rock? It means that when the storms come, you will not be blown away. Maybe you feel stable, strong, and secure but are afraid that one swift wind might just blow everything over. Your marriage has been so hard for so long. Your job has been so mundane for so many years. Things haven't been the same since the kids went to college, or since you retired, or since he died. Things happen in life that cause us to turn our ears to other voices. You think, *A little wind right now and I'm toast. A house on built on solid rock? That's not me.*

How many of us would love to know what it feels like to be secure and to prosper? Those words often make us think about money, but that's not what I mean. I'm talking about feeling secure in your soul. I'm talking about prospering in your relationships. I'm talking about really living. Really breathing in and breathing out. Finding joy, finding meaning. That kind of life comes in connection. And connection comes in hearing Jesus' words above the noise of the world.

Mr. Hagar's Garden

When I was that kid dreaming about being a future farmer, my school bus would drop off me and my brother Andy at the end of our road. The road we lived on was too narrow and curved for a school bus to go down, much less turn around in. So, each day we had about a half-mile walk from the end of the road to our house (yes, uphill, both ways, in the snow). We enjoyed the walk, really. It was a nice decompression time after a stressful day at Gladeville Elementary School and before our long, hard afternoon of playing Nintendo games and eating Little Debbie cakes.

We learned early on, though, that there was a shortcut. A hole in a fence, made by an escaped cow (or so legend had it), allowed us to detour through Mr. Hagar's yard to our field and then to the back of our house, cutting our afternoon commute in half. To get to that fence, we had to walk right through Mr. Hagar's garden, but he didn't mind. He was a kind, gentle, retired man who wore a wide-brimmed hat and always seemed to be in his garden. This garden wasn't just a few tomato plants; it required a tractor and a lot of time. Mr. Hagar was always out there, sometimes on the tractor, sometimes walking around, sometimes sitting on a five-gallon bucket turned upside down, just looking at the rows and rows of plants.

Every year there would come a time when he would call Andy and me over and say, "They're ready." The first year we didn't know what he meant. In subsequent years we were waiting for it. "They" were Mr. Hagar's prized watermelons. In our trips through the garden, we had been watching them grow, at first white and then turning deep green with lighter green stripes. When they were ripe, Mr. Hagar let us pick the first watermelon, whichever one we wanted.

Andy and I would search for the biggest and would snap it off the vine. Then one of us would throw it onto a shoulder, and we would swap it back and forth as we ran home. We would not delay eating it. This was not saved for a Saturday party. We didn't cut it into handheld portions. We broke it open and sank our faces in. This was before the magic seedless versions we have today, and so we would look up and spit out the seeds. Our faces became covered with red juice. It dripped off our chins.

We prospered. We lived. We breathed. We exulted in the glory of fruit that was grown with careful, watchful oversight by an old man who I guess, though he never said it, loved us.

Why in the world am I telling you this? Because Mr. Hagar was careful about soil. Because Mr. Hagar understood the importance of where something is planted. Because Mr. Hagar spent hours sitting on an upside-down bucket making sure everything was just right. Mr. Hagar knew something about connection, and so Andy and I enjoyed beautiful fruit.

A New Playlist: Part 4

When Jesus called us to connection and stability, it was a repeat of an Old Testament message. One place we hear that message is in David's prayer in Psalm 1. Put this on your playlist:

> *Blessed is the one*
> *who does not walk in step with the wicked*
> *or stand in the way that sinners take*
> *or sit in the company of mockers,*
> *but whose delight is in the law of the LORD,*
> *and who meditates on his law day and night.*
> *That person is like a tree planted by streams of water,*
> *which yields its fruit in season*
> *and whose leaf does not wither—*
> *whatever they do prospers.*
>
> *(Psalm 1:1-3)*

The truly happy person loves God's words and recites them day and night. The happy person puts God's words on repeat! That person is like a tree, planted by streams of water, that bears fruit and whose leaves don't fade. Similar to the house on the rock, the tree is placed where it will prosper. Its proximity to the stream is no mistake. The tree is connected to its source.

Here is what Jesus' playlist has to say about connection:

Connection requires intentionality.

I assume you are not being forced to read this book. OK, maybe a spouse or a friend gave it to you. But by making it to chapter 6 you have been intentional, and connection requires intentionality.

Connection isn't just about duty, but delight.

Duty is good. (Though I have to spell the word when I talk about it at my church, because once a preteen had to be escorted out of the sanctuary, giggling hysterically, after I said it too many times.) D-U-T-Y is good. We do some things because we are supposed to, even when we don't feel like it. But think of that tree. Its location by the stream wasn't about duty, but delight at being near the source of life. What would it look like for you to begin a journey from duty to delight? The invitation from Jesus is about something deeper than obligation; it's about getting to a place of delight.

There's no formula for connection.

With a playlist, sometimes you need a song over and over again. Sometimes you go right to a certain song that's needed for today. Sometimes you just push *play* and see where it leads. A good playlist isn't formulaic. It's about listening. It's about connecting.

Ask any farmer. Watch Mr. Hagar. There is no formula. There are practices. There are things you do time and again. But you always have time sitting on that upside-down bucket, listening and watching.

I don't have a formula for you. But there's something you can do to connect. Sit and listen to Jesus.

Connection Can Be Scary

Connection is crucial, but it can still be scary. If you build your house on rock, the winds will still blow. The rains will still come. For people who have a firm foundation, there are still risks and moments of doubt.

Rachel and I recently drove up to a retreat being held by teenagers from our church. It was the final weekend for those who were in confirmation. Confirmation is a journey in which our students learn more about the basics of faith and what it means to follow Jesus and be connected to God and the church.

When we arrived, we were told that if we moved quickly we might be able to see Mary, our oldest daughter, who would be one of the last to finish the zip line. We drove to the top of a hill and made the short hike through the woods, following the sounds of laughter (or screams of terror, we weren't sure which). We found Mary, along with several other students, standing on a platform in the top of the tallest trees. When I looked at Rachel, her face was white. Mary was unclipping from the line above her head. I knew that when you change lines, and you unclip from one and clip to the other, you always have a second, separate clip that stays fastened to a safety line. I explained this to Rachel, but it didn't seem to help her. I laughed because Rachel was so scared. But I have to admit, when Mary stepped off that platform to zip-line across the forest, my knees literally went weak.

What I realize now, thinking about it rationally, is that the most dangerous thing wouldn't have been zipping down that metal cord dozens of feet above the ground. It wouldn't have been if Mary had started dancing on the platform, or if she had been blindfolded, or even if she had jumped. All those would have been exponentially safer than one thing: if she had been disconnected from the safety line. It was all about connection.

In John 15, Jesus is moments from being arrested. He is hours from hanging on a cross. And yet, he gives one of his longest discourses, rivaling only the Sermon on the Mount. It's there that Jesus stresses the importance of connection above all else:

> *"I am the vine; you are the branches. If you*
> *remain in me and I in you, you will bear much*
> *fruit; apart from me you can do nothing."*
> *(John 15:5)*

The most dangerous thing won't be for you to jump; in fact, Jesus will ask you to jump! It won't be to dance high on a limb; I would guess Jesus hopes you dance. The true risk is when you hear Jesus' words and don't put them into practice. Of all the things you could do, the most dangerous would be to disconnect from Jesus.

Abiding with Jesus

There are many translations of John 15, and some of them, instead of *remain*, use the word *abide*. Abide in me and I in you.

Abide is not a word we use all that much, but it's a good one when we think about listening to Jesus' playlist. *Abide* means to stay, to live, or to dwell.

In this book, we've read many of Jesus' words from the beautiful playlist he offers us in this noisy world. So much of what he sings invites us to a connection that is abiding. He calls us to stay close so that we can hear his words and dwell with him.

With that in mind, here are a few last thoughts about the new playlist that Jesus has prepared for us.

A new playlist is less about doing and more about being.

Do you have a checklist of things to accomplish each day? I do! Even on weekends I'll make a list, and it makes me feel great to check things off the list. But abiding is more about being than doing. Jesus didn't come to earth so you would do this and do that and get it all done. He said he came so you could live. He is way more interested in who you are than what you do. And yet, so often I try to find my worth in what I do. I work hard. I love my job. But abiding is about being, not doing, and until we get that we will do and do and do and come up wanting.

A new playlist involves pruning.

If we accept Jesus' image of him as vine and us as branches, then we need to talk about pruning. Mr. Hagar would tell us that every branch that bears fruit needs to be pruned so it will be more fruitful. Jesus won't let us stay the same! We would love it if we could just get to a certain level with God, and then God would be done with us. But that's not how it works. Pruning is essential. It leads to healthy growth. But, you guessed it, pruning hurts! Is anybody hurting right now? Is it possible you aren't a complete failure, but that you're being pruned for something new? I don't know if it's true for you—I'm not the gardener—but I do know he's not done with you.

A new playlist is all about loving.

Jesus said, "As the Father has loved me, so I have loved you; abide in my love" (John 15:9 NRSV). Abiding is all about us knowing God's love and sharing God's love. We've said that abiding is more about being than doing, but it's not without action on our part, and that action is love. The outward expression of listening to Jesus' playlist is love. That's the fruit.

A new playlist is less about surviving and more about thriving.

Some days and some seasons in life are about surviving. You may be in one of those seasons right now. If so, the counsel is the same: stay connected. But life isn't just about making it through. Remember Psalm 1—we get to prosper! A house built on rock doesn't just make it through the storm; it stands strong for a generation.

It's probably true of all professions, but when Rachel and I were getting started in ministry, we made an interesting finding. We actively sought out pastors and their spouses who were further along the journey than we were, and we began to see a repeated pattern. Whether the ministry was deemed successful or not, it appeared that many folks went down one of two paths.

On one path were leaders who had become sort of a doormat. They were affected by every whim of every person. They were hanging on for retirement. And on the other path were leaders who were strong, but maybe too strong. No one was going to take advantage of them. They seemed to be jerks some of the time. They felt that they had to, in order to make it through the day.

Of course, those on both paths were just trying to survive, but the results were not good. Either they let people run all over them, or no one would touch them.

One day a few years into starting the new church, I had a bad day. A really bad day. I was hurting, and someone had hurt me. I came into the kitchen after what felt like a verbal boxing match that I had just lost. I began telling Rachel how I felt and exactly how I was going to handle it. I could tell by the look on her face that she thought I was being a donkey. Of course, I remembered our many talks about pastors being either doormats or jerks, and so did she.

Rachel said, "I'm praying for you to be a third way." I told her I didn't need her to be spiritual right now. But I also said, "Yeah, what's that?" She said, "I'm praying that you stay connected. I'm praying that you abide."

That's the way Jesus invites us to go. We are armed with a playlist that says we have to do everything and please everyone, but Jesus says, "Not so fast." Like, really, you don't have to go that fast. Jesus stopped because he cared about our hearts, and we can stop, too. We can stop and listen.

Our world says, "Get mad or get run over." We show that attitude at work, in our relationships, and on social media. We can choose that approach, but it's the way of sand. A new playlist tells us to stay, to stay connected to Jesus, like a branch to a vine. A different fruit grows out of us. That fruit is love.

What Jesus modeled was not a doormat but a strong, humble King who went where God led even when it hurt. He died. But, you know the story, not for long.

On the third day, Mary went to the tomb, because where else would you go? And Jesus' body was gone. Someone came up behind her. It was Jesus. He was alive. His life meant that Mary could have life. His coming close to her in that season of death meant there's nowhere we can go that will be outside the reach of his voice.

I'm trying to go slower, be quieter, love more. I'm trying to listen. And when I do, I hear the voice of the one who gives me life. You can, too.

NOTES

Chapter 2. Who Is Your Master?

1. Alex Soojung-Kim Pang, *The Distraction Addiction: Getting the Information You Need and the Communication You Want, Without Enraging Your Family, Annoying Your Colleagues, and Destroying Your Soul* (New York: Little Brown and Company, 2013).

2. "House Divided Speech" (Speech by Abraham Lincoln at Illinois Republican State Convention, Springfield, Illinois, June 16, 1858), The History Place, http://www.historyplace.com/lincoln/divided.htm. Accessed November 14, 2017.

Chapter 4. Rule Followers, Rule Breakers

1. T. B. Larimore, "Chapter XII: Sermon—The Iron Rule, the Silver Rule, and the Golden Rule" in *Letters and Sermons of T. B. Larimore*, ed. F. D. Srygley (Nashville: McQuiddy Printing Company, 1903), 213-233, https://digitalcommons.acu.edu/crs_books/100/. Accessed November 29, 2017.

2. Wayne Jackson, "Three Rules of Human Conduct," http://www.apologeticspress.org/APContent.aspx?category=97&article=265. Accessed November 1, 2017.

Chapter 5. The Right Words

1. Joseph Epstein, *Narcissus Leaves the Pool: Essays by Joseph Epstein* (Boston: Mariner Books, reprint 2007), 80.

2. Eugene H. Peterson, *As Kingfishers Catch Fire: A Conversation on the Ways of God Formed by the Words of God* (New York: WaterBrook, 2017), 197.

ACKNOWLEDGMENTS

Thank you to my playlist:

John, Paul, George, and Ringo, thank you for putting that beat in my heart when I was kid.

Bob Dylan, thank you for teaching me as a seventeen-year-old that "he not busy being born is busy dying."

Paul Simon, I will never forget that we are all going to Graceland.

Tom Petty (whom we lost last year), thanks for giving me *Wildflowers* as the first CD I put in my first stereo. I haven't been the same since.

Andrew Peterson, your songs are the soundtrack of my inner life. Thank you for "The Dark Before the Dawn." It pulled me out of a cave this past year.

Rich Mullins, thanks for teaching me that if I sing, I sing for the joy that has born in me these songs.

Audrey Assad, thank you for leading me in worship every Saturday night before I lead folks in worship on Sunday.

Providence Church, I love to sing with you the old and new hymns of the church and hear them echo off the walls of the sanctuary and of our hearts. Thank you for sharing your voice with me and with so many who need hope, healing, and wholeness.

Providence Worship Band—Jenny, Jeana, and the whole gang—you are my favorite band, and I am so fortunate to get caught up in worship with you week after week.

Dad, falling asleep to your guitar and waking up to the piano in our house shaped who I am. You are, to me, the greatest living songwriter.

Mom, thanks for singing James Taylor over me at night and now over my girls. You taught us to close our eyes and know it's all right.

My girls—Mary, Lydia, and Phoebe—keep singing songs of truth and power and light. The world needs your voices.

Dolly Parton, I will always love you.

Rachel, I will always love you more than Dolly. My favorite song is the one we have written together.

Jesus—you who have sung over me in the dark and in the light—I can't wait to sing with you forever. May every song point to you and give you glory, honor, and praise.

The Connected Life
Small Groups That Create Community

This handy and helpful guide describes how churches can set up, maintain, and nurture small groups to create a congregation that is welcoming and outward-looking.

Written by founding pastor Jacob Armstrong with Rachel Armstrong, the guide is based on the pioneering small group ministry of Providence United Methodist Church in Mt. Juliet, Tennessee.

978-1-5018-4345-7
978-1-5018-4346-4 eBook

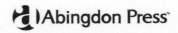

Available wherever fine books are sold.